NORTON
ROTARIES

NORTON ROTARIES

Kris Perkins

OSPREY
AUTOMOTIVE

FOR
SEAN AND ARAN

Published in 1991 by Osprey Publishing Limited
59 Grosvenor Street, London W1X 9DA

© Kris Perkins

Cataloguing in Publication Data is
available from the British Library

ISBN 1855321 81 5

Editor Shaun Barrington
Page design Gwyn Lewis
Phototypeset by Keyspools Limited
Printed by BAS Printers Limited
Over Wallop, Hampshire

FRONT COVER Trevor Nation tests the suspension on the
JPS water-cooled Norton in 1990.

BACK COVER F1 in lilac at the 1990 International
Motorcycle Show, Birmingham.

HALF TITLE Pre-race preparation of the Norton rotary
race machine.

TITLE PAGE Steve Spray, whose efforts attracted the
black and gold sponsorship of JPS.

For a catalogue of all books published by Osprey Automotive
please write to:

The Marketing Department,
Octopus Illustrated Books, 1st Floor, Michelin House,
81 Fulham Road, London SW3 6RB

Contents

Acknowledgements

My special thanks go to Mrs Jean Wilson for all her patient hours of research and help in writing this book. I would also like to express my gratitude to Mark Pinfield and the following individuals of Norton for their time and assistance during the production of this book:

Philippe Le Roux OBE; Graham Williams; Tony Denniss; David Garside; Doug Hele; Bob Rowley; Bob Haynes and Melanie Rock; Barry Symmons and Julie O'Neal, Norton Racing; Brian Crighton; Trevor Nation; Steve Spray; Chris Mehew; Dave Evans; Dave Hickman; Chris Pike; Ray Corbett; Tony Bass; Richard Negus. Thanks must also go to the following: Paul Hadley, Paul Fowler and Neil Webster of Action Media International Ltd; Dave Boon, Race Coordinator NGK Spark Plugs; Steve Kenward of Heron Suzuki PLC; Peter Bolt and Jenny Chantrell of Motor Cycle News; Thorn – EMI Electronics Ltd; Colin Rust – Rust Racing; Michael Hugh George and Richard Waterhouse of the Royal Automobile Club; Ivan Shaw, Aviation Composites Ltd; Bill Yates, Bob Holland, Safety Regulations Group Civil Aviation Authority; Lancing Marine; Norton Owners Club; Mazda; Roy Richards and Dave Roach of The National Motorcycle Museum; Tony Holt; Sue Richardson; Brian Woolley of *Classic Motorcycle*. Last but not least to my editor Mr Nicholas Collins whose idea this book was.

Photographs by:

The Author; Action Media; G W Aldridge; Chris Mehew; Mike Rushton; Norton Motors (1978) Ltd; EMAP and Motor Cycle News; Eric Cavill; Don Morley; John Noble; Tony Denniss.

Introduction

The development of the Norton rotary engine has taken place over a relatively short period of time, in comparison to the long-established reciprocal engine. This development period has been marked by industrial disputes, recession, lack of investment and the shrinking of the motorcycle market. Yet despite all the problems it has had to face, the rotary engine has become the focus of the Norton resurrection.

This book looks at the historical background to the Norton company and then goes on to consider the evolution of the company's rotary motorcycles. It traces the story from initial experiments, to see if the engine was viable for use in a motorcycle, to the production of the F1 Superbike.

Running parallel to the road bike production has been the development of the Norton rotary race machines. This has aroused fervent support from the race fans, obviously pleased to see a British-made bike challenging the Japanese machinery. With its success has come controversy, as many arguments rage over the capacity of the rotary engine.

This story is not ended, as development of the engine still continues; nor would it be complete unless some mention was made of the people, some named in this book, many others anonymous, who have contributed so much to the development of this exciting engine.

Kris Perkins

Foreword

When Dennis Poore and the team at Norton committed the company to the rotary engine in the 1970s, they could not have envisaged the tortuous route that the company would follow to bring the rotary into production. Nor could they have anticipated the quantum leaps which the Japanese manufacturers would make in the intervening period. Today, the Norton aficionado could be forgiven for wondering whether it has all been worthwhile.

The vision for Norton, which I inherited from Dennis Poore, was to produce a revolutionary motorcycle based on the rotary engine, which would be as light as a 250cc and have the power of a 750cc. This is now essentially achievable, if not with the F1, then certainly with the next generation of motorcycles. What has changed since the 1970s is the market requirement, which means that this strategy must be modified.

If the motorcycle is to survive into the next century as a road vehicle, then it must become more practical and user-friendly than it is at present. I believe that Norton, with its compact and powerful rotary engine, is well positioned to challenge successfully the basic assumptions of modern motorcycle design. The strategy should no longer be confined to more powerful, lighter machines.

The challenge for Norton, the manufacturer, is not only how to beat last year's number no.1 motorcycle. It is how to compete with the small car. If Norton is to exploit its advantages with the rotary, it must focus on this competitor for consumer spending. To be successful in this market, the future motorcycle must significantly out-perform the modern four wheeler as a means of transporting people (and goods) from A to B.

Once we have caught up with where Norton should have been ten years ago, namely with a light, powerful and reliable rotary motorcycle, we can start developing machines for the 21st century that take account of our diminishing natural resources; the sort of machines which will be essential if people are to have any hope of retaining the great luxury of personal vehicles.

Norton is half way through its strategy as a modern motorcycle manufacturer. It has proven its unique rotary engine, both in the market and on the race track (as is amply

demonstrated by this book). But this is only half the solution. If Norton is ever to appeal to the mass market again, as opposed to the dedicated enthusiast, (and that is surely the key to survival) it must concentrate on producing competitive commuter vehicles in which both rider and passenger can feel safe, warm, dry and comfortable and can save time, money and scarce resources in comparison with using a small car for any given journey. To ensure Norton's future, nothing less will do.

Here at last is the book that answers all the questions about the Norton rotary engines and my JPS race machine. I am particularly interested in the background history of the rotary engine as we are at the forefront of its development, and here it is set out in full. With Norton at present being the only British marque involved in competition with the Japanese, I take great pride in being part of it.

Whether you are an ardent race supporter or an armchair follower, I am sure you will find *Norton Rotaries* fascinating reading. It contains something for everyone, the race enthusiast, the motorcyclist, the engineering technology fan.

A Brief History of Norton

In 1898 James Landsdowne Norton, better known as 'Pa' Norton, founded the Norton Manufacturing Company. By 1913 the company had changed its name to Norton Motors Ltd and was making motorcycles at Bradford Street in Birmingham.

The first motorcycles were powered by Moto-Réve engines from Switzerland, but built under manufacturing licence in Britain. French Peugeot V twin engines were used to power larger machines. One of these was raced in 1907 to a win in the first Isle of Man Tourist Trophy, twin cylinder class by Rem (short for Rembrandt) H Fowler. Rem bought the machine and paid his own entry fees. In the race, despite a number of stops, including one lasting 22 minutes to repair a burst front tyre, Rem won at an average speed of 36.22 mph and achieved the fastest lap at 42.91 mph.

Although Rem Fowler received his prize money for this win, he did not receive a trophy until 1957, when he was presented with a genuine TT replica from the Vintage Motor Cycle Club in recognition of his pioneering feat. Thus began the long association of Norton with the Isle of Man Tourist Trophy races.

A series of large capacity machines followed, such as the 633 cc side valve single produced in 1907, a 490 cc model in 1911 and in 1922 the first factory-built overhead valve single. During this time of expansion, around 4,500 machines a year were being produced; as a result the factory moved to new premises at Bracebridge Street, Aston, Birmingham.

In 1924 Norton won the Senior TT with Alec Bennett and also won the sidecar TT with George Tucker and factory technician, Walter William Moore. This triumph was overshadowed by the death of James L Landsdowne Norton, the founder of the Norton marque, who died unexpectedly at the age of 56.

1925 saw the arrival of an Irishman and former racer, Joe Craig, who took over the racing department. The following year the first 348 cc Norton went into production, a racing model for the TT. In the mid-1920s Norton were highly successful with their overhead valve engines and there seemed to be little reason for change until 1926. Rumours that the competition were to produce an overhead cam engine were proven correct when another manufacturer won the TT with this type of engine. This prompted Joe Craig to direct Walter William Moore, a talented designer, who had a proven record with work on developing ohv engines for racing, to develop an ohc engine. By 1927, Norton had their own ohc engine and with this they proceeded to dominate the TT that year with riders Alec Bennett and Stanley Woods. These machines had demonstrated two Norton attributes to the public: speed and reliability. Both factors helped to justify racing as a means of selling production models to the public.

In 1928, in keeping with their strategy of offering the previous season's race models in production version, Norton released the CS1 as their first ohc 500 model for the sum of £89. At the TT that year a slimmed down version of the overhead cam engine, a 350cc model, was raced unsuccessfully. The following year this model was released as the CJ1 (Camshaft Junior) but this again was not a good year for Norton as they had little racing success.

Walter Moore then left to work for NSU in Germany, and it fell to the new designer Arthur Carroll (brought in by Joe Craig) to redesign and improve the overhead cam engine by integrating many of the successful Velocette design principles. From this point on, for nearly thirty years, the Norton ohc engine was referred to as the Carroll engine. By 1931 this engine was the basis for the factory race machines which had a good Isle of Man TT that year and led to the production of the Model 30, 490cc and Model 40, 348cc Internationals. Over the years these machines were steadily improved. The model 30 International of 1938 was a single cylinder, overhead cam, four stroke engine of 490 cc (79×100 mm). It featured a $3\frac{3}{4}$-gallon fuel tank, a 3.00×21-in front tyre and 3.25×20-in rear. Top speed was an estimated 82 mph. The machine cost £93.

In 1935 Jimmy Guthrie raised the One Hour speed record to 183.5 km/h (114 mph) at Montlhery in France on a 500 cc Norton single. One of the modifications introduced during 1936 was rear springing. That must have come as some relief to the riders, for the roads were very bumpy in those days. Another tentative step forward was made the following year when Joe Craig introduced a twin overhead cam engine following the lead of Norton's rivals, Velocette, but it did not meet expectations and was shelved until 1938.

During this time Norton was the machine to race and was the most successful English make of motorcycle, known throughout the world. In addition, to the road machines, Norton also released two Racing Inter-

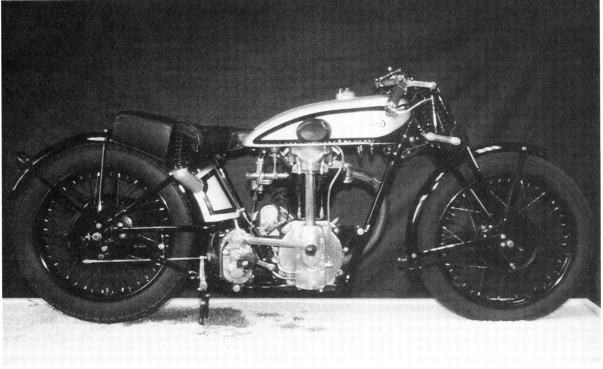

TOP **Rem Fowler's 1907 Norton Twin TT-winning machine.**

BOTTOM **The CS1, first released in 1928: the designation stood for Cam Shaft 1.**

TOP **1932 Norton 350 cc Manx model 40.**   BOTTOM **Model 30 International.**

1955 Norton Dominator, 500 cc model 88, from Herbert Hopwood's original design.

national models which were the forerunners of the Manx machines. These featured alloy engines, a racing magneto, race carburettor and a close-ratio gearbox, a superb machine for its time. However Norton officially retired from racing in 1939 giving the reasons that it was too disruptive to their road machine production and that they were now commited to fulfilling contracts from the services. From 1939 to late 1945 the Norton factory turned out over 100,000 motorcycles for the armed services and these were used in many theatres of war·in a number of different guises.

In 1946 the factory resumed production of civilian motorcycles. The first models produced were similar to the pre-war machines as the need was for high production figures rather than development. After the war motorcycling was more popular with the general public and sales increased. But for the man on the street, from 1946 to 1948, all that he could get were the dated long stroke single overhead cam engines long abandoned by the factory race machines. The Manx Norton racing machine appeared prior to the Manx Grand Prix that September. A number of the new machines appeared on the grid. Norton had returned to its pre-war policy (if indeed there was a policy) of putting its major effort into racing, using the factory machines as test beds for ideas for the production models. When racing resumed, riders such as Geoff Duke, Mike Hailwood and John Surtees leapt to fame with numerous wins on Manx Nortons.

The postwar market was developing in the more prosperous United States, where racing success helped boost sales. For Norton the late 1940s and early 1950s looked promising. Herbert Hopwood, who had joined Norton in 1947, designed two new production models, a 497 cc ohv vertical twin – later to become the Dominator – and a 490 cc ohv single for trials. In addition he instigated various improvements to the highly successful ohc racing Manx models.

To further improve the machines Joe Craig brought in the expertise of the Irish brothers Rex and Cromie McCandless, specialist frame makers, to improve the frame and suspension systems. Their work led to the production of the Featherbed Norton in 1950, so-called because of the smooth ride afforded by the pivoted fork rear suspension. This became one of the most famous and successful race machines ever.

But Norton were already making the mistake of investing too much money in their racing ventures rather than in developing new factory facilities. This was borne out by Herbert Hopwood who felt that the management did not appear to realise that it was commercial suicide to have racing as a first priority. He had estimated that for a long time the company had been devoting almost all of its meagre resources to

1962 Norton Manx 30M 500 cc with featherbed frame, produced at the AMC factory, Plumstead.

racing rather than development of road machines. The few changes that were made to the road machines were mainly minor alterations. (Though from 1953 onwards all Norton motorcycles came equipped with swinging fork rear suspension instead of the dated plunger type system, and many models also featured the famous Featherbed frame.)

1953 was significant in the history of Norton as it saw the takeover of the company by Associated Motor Cycles (AMC) of London, who already owned AJS and Matchless motorcycles. Joe Craig, who had done so much development work for Norton, retired in 1955 but was tragically killed in a car accident two years later. Bert Hopwood returned to the factory as technical manager during 1955 along with Doug Hele. They produced the Dominator 88, followed in 1956 by the Dominator 99. Both machines were vertical twins featuring duplex-loop, all-welded frames similar to the Manx featherbed frames of the racers; these frames were often referred to as wideline, as the top frame tubes meant that the seat was uncomfortably wide at the front. It was not until 1960 that the frame was narrowed allowing a slimline, more comfortable seat unit to be used.

In 1958 the Norton marque celebrated its sixtieth birthday by producing a 249 cc parallel twin with forward facing sloping cylinders called, not surprisingly, the Jubilee. The development of the Jubilee turned out to be a very wise decision, for during 1960

the government introduced a capacity limitation for learners of a maximum of 250 cc. This obviously helped the promotion of sales for this particular machine. For those with a full licence there was the larger capacity version of the Jubilee, the 350 cc Navigator. At this point Bert Hopwood was promoted to managing director of the company and immediately started to streamline the concern, cut costs and improve the image of the machines by exploiting the publicity garnered from the racing success of the Manx Nortons. During the 1961 TT races a young Mike Hailwood won the Senior race on a privately entered single at over 100 mph.

During 1962 under the AMC ownership scheme, to concentrate production and help stave off impending bankruptcy, the Norton company was moved from its home at Bracebridge Street in Birmingham, to London, to the AMC factory at Plumstead. From here a 648 cc vertical twin and also a 745 cc version machine, the Atlas, were produced for the general market. The last batch of the famous 499 cc Manx were also completed. This period saw a loss of identity for Norton. The new factory and largely new workforce, (only five of the original work force moved south) meant that the machines became more and more a mixture of Norton, AJS and Matchless. The factory machinery from

Birmingham had all been moved to the Plumstead site and for a number of reasons never seemed to produce such good results as they had previously, so that quality became a problem.

By August 1966 AMC Ltd ceased production and the company was put in the hands of a receiver. But on September 2 the complete holdings, including Norton, were bought up by Dennis Poore who owned Manganese Bronze Holdings (MBH). Manganese Bronze Holdings were the parent company for a group of mechanical engineering and metal manufacturing firms. They also included the Villiers motorcycle company, which Poore had bought the year before. The motorcycle interests of MBH thus became known as Norton-Villiers.

Cutbacks on production were made and the factory was limited to the making of 650 cc and 746 cc ohv twins, the majority of which were sent for export to the United States. The export of machines to the US tripled over the three-year period from 1962 to 1965 and sales forecasts indicated that the American market would be buying around 750,000 motorcycles a year by 1967. Sales were therefore, not surprisingly, concentrated on this expanding market.

Project P10: The Commando

This period also witnessed the sad end of the few survivors of the British motorcycle industry: Cotton, DMW, Greeves, James, Francis-Barnet and Royal Enfield. Two years later the engine production plant was transferred to the old Villiers engine factory in Wolverhampton that had been acquired earlier by Dennis Poore. Under this cloud of despondency in the industry, Dennis Poore took the initiative and convened a meeting of the executives from the Norton, Matchless and Villiers plants. At the meeting he gave the group its target, to produce a model to act as the flagship of the new concern, a model primarily aimed at the expanding US market but also viable for the UK. The deadline for the prototype was the September 1967 Earls Court Motorcycle Show. The project was coded P10 and was headed by Bernard Hooper, an experienced designer and development engineer from Villiers.

The starting point for the project was an old design by Charles Udall who five years earlier had designed an 800 cc dohc parallel twin featuring a unit-built four-speed gearbox. The original idea had a modified Featherbed frame to house the heavy engine in a forward tilted position. Development of this project began with work on the engine but progress was soon halted by the news that work on the existing Atlas engine had produced more power than the new one would be able to match; allied to the fact that vibration seemed particularly bad from the new design.

Early in 1967, Dr Stefan Bauer joined the company from Rolls-Royce as Director of Engineering. He soon made it clear that the design as it stood was simply unacceptable for the envisaged flagship of the company. Dennis Poore terminated the project with only three months remaining before the show, still determined to launch a new machine.

Hooper, who was equally disillusioned with the project, hit upon the idea of exploiting the Atlas engine in a modified frame. Instead of using the renowned Featherbed frame, attention was focussed on using a frame with a single top tube, in fact a 2.25-in diameter main spine member, twin forward down tubes and a triangulated rear sub-frame. This new frame was substantially lighter at 24 lb than the Featherbed frame which was around 35 lb. The problem of vibration had been given considerable thought and the solution was to isolate the rider by hanging the engine, gearbox and rear swinging arm from the frame using rubber bushes. The idea worked and the term 'Isolastic' was born.

Within the original deadline (the motorcycle show at Earls Court) the project team had produced their prototype despite that near disastrous false start. The name given to the machine was one that had already been used by the AMC-owned James company in 1960 for a 250 cc two stroke scrambler machine, 'Commando'.

The Commando prototype featured a modified Atlas engine of 750 cc, inclined forward in the new frame. The overall colour of the machine was silver with a bright orange seat and finished at the back by an unusual tapered seat unit. The machine looked aggressive enough to live up to its name and weighed in at 430 lb kerb weight. The race-styled seat unit gave rise to the model name 'Fastback'. Performance from the Commando was equally impressive. Acceleration was given as 0 to 60 mph in around five seconds and from 0 to 100 mph in under twelve seconds.

The company now had a fixed objective with the production of the Commando at the Plumstead site. Enthusiasm for the new model resulted in around 4,000 machines being produced during 1968. The majority of these machines went for export, as the Commando had achieved international acclaim very quickly, especially in the United States. It appeared that Dennis Poore had achieved his ambition for a new competitive model that was going to be a market killer and hopefully the salvation of the company.

To compound the success Dennis Poore decided to cash in on the lucrative fleet sales market by supplying the police traffic department with motorcycles. To achieve this he recruited the existing Triumph police motorcycle fleet manager Neale Shilton to develop and market a suitable Norton machine. Work on this project began at Woolwich but was later transferred to the Andover site where the police Norton, the Interpol, was produced.

Financial difficulties continued on the home market resulting in a slump of new machine sales in the UK.

Sales dwindled so much that by 1972 the majority of sales were going abroad, largely to the United States.

The company was plagued by continuing problems such as a lack of unity among internal company divisions and the familiar bugbear to development, the lack of (or the reluctance of management to invest) adequate money. Cost cutting exercises were still the vogue for maintaining financial stability and as a result the factory spares and service facilities at Plumstead were closed.

By March 1969 the company was producing two further versions of the Commando. The range now included the 750 Fastback MkII, the 750 'S' type and the 750 Roadster MkI.

The early success with the Commando now began to bring its own problems, with many machines suffering from electrical faults, porous castings or main bearing failure. The majority of these faults were not attributable to design mistakes but to production policy. The company had hit upon a good machine and wanted to cash in on the sales. Quality control went out of the window in the demand for higher production figures, most of the demand coming from export. It became more and more evident that MBH expected more profit from its investment in the motorcycle industry and to achieve this they were prepared to sacrifice quality for quantity.

1969 saw the closure of the Woolwich factory following a compulsory purchase order from the GLC.

1969, Norton Commando 750 cc: This is just one of the model variations produced that year.

At the same time the Plumstead factory was also being run down. On July 25 1969 the last Woolwich-built Commando, a 750 'S' model, left the assembly plant. The remaining site at Wolverhampton was designated the engine assembly plant for the Commando with the machine assembly plant located 130 miles to the south on an industrial site in Walworth, London! A new company base would be established on a modern government-sponsored development at Andover in Hampshire near the Thruxton race circuit.

Production at Andover began with a steady 30 machines a day but as the work force gained in experience this gradually rose to around 60 machines. The unusual move to Andover had obviously had some purpose behind it for a test and development department was soon established at the Thruxton race circuit and in February 1970 it was announced that Norton-Villiers were to produce a number of tuned, production race machines equipped with disc brakes.

One reason for the return to racing was that Dennis Poore had a long-held ambition to re-establish a Norton race team. Another was that the company felt the glamour of racing would have a positive effect on the sales of machines. In addition, the factory had been involved for some time with Dunstall in producing

ABOVE **John Player sponsored race machine.**

RIGHT **750 cc Norton Challenge.**

tuning kits and parts for racing. Over the two previous years, several racers had been successful. Ray Pickerell, had won the first 750 cc Production TT race on the Isle of Man in June 1968 on a Dunstall Norton. In 1969, Mick Andrews had won the Hutchinson 100 race, (run the 'wrong way' round the circuit) at Brands Hatch on a Commando; and Paul Smart had ridden a Norton to second place in the 750 Production TT.

The production race machine that was produced was the 750 cc Norton PR. This machine owed much of its success to a new man at Andover in the development team, Peter Williams. Like many of his predecessors Peter Williams was an extremely talented development engineer and he was also a highly skilled road racer.

In addition to the production racer the factory also offered a high performance option for the 750 cc engine. This up-rated engine was called the Combat engine and was available from 1970.

Using contacts from his car racing days, Dennis Poore sought and managed to secure a sponsor for a Norton motorcycle race team to compete again. In November 1971 the race team was launched and the sponsor revealed as the Imperial Tobacco Company. This was a breakthrough, as the first sponsorship deal involving a company outside the industry. The team was launched as the John Player Norton race team. The colours of the John Player logo were a suitably patriotic red, white and blue. After a long break, the Norton name was once again seen on the race circuits.

But all was not well within the Norton-Villiers concern as the reliability problems of the Commando grew steadily worse. In a desperate attempt to bolster falling sales of the Commando, the strengthened engine, the Combat, was introduced from January 1972 as standard fitment to a new model, the Interstate. The machine also featured a large petrol tank holding around $5\frac{1}{2}$ gallons and featured disc brakes as fitted on the race bikes. To counter the growing reliability problem with the Commando, the company decided to fit the Combat engine to all Commando models (apart from the Hi-Rider) from October 1972.

1972 brought further bad news to the ailing British motorcycle industry. The BSA-Triumph group at Meriden in Coventry, Norton-Villiers only real rivals, was facing mounting debts despite launching a range of new machines and showing reasonable sales figures. The reason for the Norton-Villiers and BSA-Triumph decline was, of course, the increasing pressure from Japan. In simple terms the government-supported motor cycle industry in Japan was able to produce cheaper, more modern machines at a faster rate.

Twin-cylinder machines like the Commando were being superseded by the new Japanese four-cylinder machines. The Commando was near the limit of engine power production, whereas the four cylinder engines gave large scope for expansion in power tuning. The industry had to face the fact that they couldn't match the volume or quality of the Japanese machinery. Prices were marginally cheaper for these imported machines.

Norton-Villiers-Triumph: Bigger is Better?

At this time BSA-Triumph finally reached rock bottom. Against a background of industrial unrest and strikes, with debts of over half a million pounds, they turned to the government for financial help and approached the Department of Trade and Industry. It wasn't until the end of the year that the DTI intimated that it would consider investing around £20 million in the industry to try to save it from collapse. There were provisos though: the DTI obviously thought that Dennis Poore's Norton-Villiers company was more solvent than it actually was, and that he was the man who might be able to save the industry. They therefore agreed to provide the capital if Norton-Villiers and BSA-Triumph amalgamated, with Dennis Poore as the chairman.

So in early 1973 Norton-Villiers-Triumph (NVT) was born, with the government holding a substantial stake, to form the mainstay of the British motorcycle industry. Work at the factories continued with Norton-Villiers at Wolverhampton and Andover, BSA at Small Heath and Triumph at Meriden.

In February that year Norton-Villiers released the Mark five version of the Commando. A lot of work had been done on this machine by the development department at Wolverhampton. Work had been concentrated on the improvement of reliability and had included an up-rated head gasket, raised gear ratio, improved ignition system and bearings. The application and success of these improvements was dependent upon the purchase of new expensive factory machinery. Change-over of machinery was time consuming and severely reduced production at this time.

The beginning of the year also saw the launch of the new 850 MkI Commando which appeared in March; an Interstate, Roadster and a Hi-Rider version were also available. High hopes rested on the new 850: it was believed that the recurrent reliability problems of the 750 had finally been cleared. Later the same year NVT launched a limited edition of the Commando styled along café-racer lines and finished in the John Player racing team colours.

At the time of the amalgamation many development projects came to light; among them a project coded P41. For some time at BSA, work had been going on to build a road machine based upon the unusual Wankel rotary

engine. There were many problems still to be resolved . . .

At Norton Dennis Poore had other plans for the future; one was the development of a new twin cylinder water-cooled racing machine that would then replace the Commando. Development work on this new engine, the Challenge, would be carried out with the racing car engine experts Cosworth. Again, Norton appeared to be basing their future on the success of a racing motorcycle design. Work began in September 1973 and they hoped to race the machine during 1975; but it would take a further two years at least before a road version could be available. This was obviously far too long. The lack of long-term planning within the British motorcycle industry can be easily criticised with hindsight, but it should also be remembered that this was a time of acute financial and industrial insecurity.

1973 saw the start of the political problems that were to plague NVT over the following years. The first of these was the involuntary redundancy of 100 workers at the Andover assembly plant. Four years previously Norton had obliged a number of these men to move south from Woolwich or lose their jobs. Later in September a dispute at Meriden started to bleed NVT of around £20,000 a week, disrupted production of machines at Small Heath and very severely affected company finances.

On the racing side, the year turned out to be one of the best for the John Player Norton team as Peter

Williams set a new lap record at Brands Hatch alongside Barry Sheene on his Suzuki. In the Isle of Man TT Peter Williams won the Formula 750 race and Mick Grant came second.

Continuing poor production at Wolverhampton was increasing concern over the viability of the original plan to maintain the factory alongside the Small Heath and Meriden works. In the United States, sales continued to fall as the Japanese manufacturers began to introduce more refined machines and in sufficient quantity to undercut the price of British machines. 1974 saw the start of a 'Bike British' marketing campaign both at home and abroad, focused on the sale of the Commando and the Trident which had been inherited from Triumph.

Another Norton-Villiers project that was already underway at the time of the amalgamation was the SPX Wulf 500 twin, first built at Wolverhampton in 1973. The project was the work of Bernard Hooper and John Favill whose stepped-piston engine design was mounted in a revolutionary pressed steel monocoque frame. The frame was rumoured to be the work of Sir Alex Issigonis (who designed the Mini). A grant for the project had been received from the National Research and Development Council. This grant was not renewed the following year and the project closed in November; hopes now rested upon the P41 Wankel project.

Dennis Poore's other development plan, in addition to the Wankel project, was for the importing of small, cheap, Italian engines for use in constructing and marketing a British moped to exploit the growing market for cheap transport.

The continuing industrial dispute at the Triumph Meriden works took a new turn when the work force took things into their own hands and formed a co-operative to run the factory and keep it open. NVT were facing increasing problems all round and not surprisingly the company failed to prosper that year. Despite the commitment made earlier to support the amalgamation of the companies, the government then decided that it would support the breakaway by the Meriden co-operative. In March 1975 they agreed to make a loan of £5 million to the co-operative, in the face of protests from NVT.

During the same month the latest and what also proved to be the last models of the Commando appeared: the 850 cc MkIII Roadster and Interstate. May 1975 saw the launch of the Interpol MkIII aimed at the lucrative police market but already many police authorities had been put off by the spiralling price and doubtful future of the factory. They looked for an

LEFT **1975 850cc Mark III electric start in Manx silver trim.**

BELOW **Early prototype Wankel engine. (EMAP)**

alternative and many soon followed the example of the Avon and Somerset police by turning to BMW.

The Government was approached for a further loan but the industry was considered to be too unstable and the loan was withheld. NVT were now in severe financial difficulty further compounded by falling sales in the United States. They announced a loss of £3,700,000 for 1974. This loss was blamed largely on the dispute at Meriden which had disrupted production of the Trident.

The nadir was reached when an exasperated creditor, tired of waiting for payment, issued a summons in the high court suing for payment of £23,000 or seizure of NVT property to secure the sum. With no capital to pay this summons the company called in the liquidators and so motorcycle production ceased, apart from at the workers co-operative at Meriden.

The Wolverhampton workers returned from holiday to find liquidation of the company in progress. The unions, encouraged by local MPs, were intent on recovering outstanding wages owed to them by the company and a sit-in commenced on August 7. A large number of workers were also determined to prevent the removal of the 500 part-built Commandos remaining whilst seeking recompense. They also wanted the production of the 850 cc Commando to continue and the re-introduction of the Wulf project which they felt

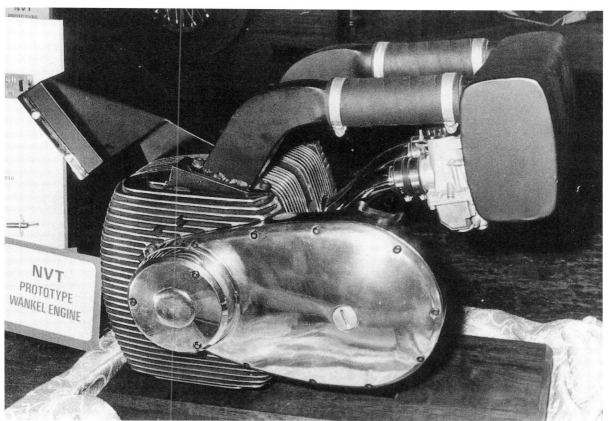

could save the factory. Development of Bernard Hooper's and John Favill's Wulf project recommenced when NRDC money was once again forthcoming, so that by September 1975 a 500 cc prototype was unveiled. Negotiations were opened by a Workers' Action Committee in an attempt to find backers for the production of the Commando and the Wulf.

The management, faced with the liquidation of NVT, only appeared interested in disposing of the blockaded Commandos and other stock as quickly and profitably as possible. It became increasingly apparent that the Meriden co-operative takeover was partly to blame for the situation that NVT now found them-

selves in. The government funds that had gone to Meriden were not available to rescue NVT, despite the fact that the police were more inclined to buy the Interpol rather than a Triumph twin.

In the meantime Bernard Hooper and John Favill had continued with development of the 850 Commando and in early 1976 they produced the Norton 76, a restyled version equipped with an SU carburettor and featuring cast alloy wheels.

Dennis Poore made it clear that he did not wish to have anything to do with orders for the Commando as he felt that it should be superseded by the Challenge. Meanwhile, towards the end of 1975 the High Court

Interpol Mk11 in RAC livery; chosen as a fleet vehicle for its reliability and promised long service life.

were told that plans to resume partial production had been approved by the government. But it was only in December 1976 that the rescue came. Joint financing with Barclays Bank allowed NVT Engineering Ltd, a new company, to be set up at the smaller Sparkbrook factory in Birmingham to allow the disposal of the stocks held overseas and provide servicing for the machines already sold. There was no commitment to NVT to continue the production of motorcycles. A

trust fund for the creditors of NVT Manufacturing Ltd was set up to help them get their money back.

Amidst the confusion, Dennis Poore put into production another of his hopes for the future, the Easy Rider moped, built at a former bacon factory at Lynn Lane, Shenstone, near Lichfield in Staffordshire. (These NVT premises soon became home to other projects including the P41 rotary, of which several promising prototypes had already been built.)

The Easy Rider ER 1 was fitted with a 49.9 cc Morini engine from Italy and a French frame. About a hundred of these were built in a week at Shenstone. Dennis Poore felt that the moped would sell well at the time of the energy crisis and he was later proved right. He also announced that NVT Motors had agreed to buy all the partly built Commandos in the factory from the liquidator. The Action Committee was still hoping for a buy-out and the sale was delayed.

Since March 1976 a hundred Interpols had been produced; in June the blockade was quietly lifted and the factory prepared to produce industrial engines again as a cash generator to make the finishing of the 500 remaining Commandos possible. During October the factory was bought by two West Midland businessmen, Mark Scull and David Sankey, who set up Wolverhampton Industrial Engines, continuing production of the industrial powerplants.

In November a number of the men got the go-ahead to build the final batch of 1,500 MkIII Commandos and in the same deal Dennis Poore bought the Norton name and manufacturing rights from the liquidator. But it wasn't the Commando that he was interested in. By September 1977 the last of the 1,500 Commandos was completed; in 1978 a further thirty machines were made at the Andover factory, and that was it.

At this point, both Bernard Hooper and John Favill realised that there would be little support for the Wulf project amidst the complex wheeling and dealing of the company struggle for survival, and both men left. The remaining BSA personnel were moved to Birmingham where general engineering contracts were serviced and where development of the Wankel engine was continuing in the experimental laboratory. The Norton spares and accessories operation was run from Andover and in the summer of 1977 this became Andover (Norton) Ltd.

Toward the end of the 1970s NVT profits from its various activities had improved sufficiently to allow the repayment in full of earlier loans and the future began to look promising. The reason for this cautious optimism was the growing success of the Wankel project operated by the motorcycle division now named Norton Motors (1978) Ltd. A number of prototypes had already been produced with good press reaction.

The Mark I appeared in 1979 and 25 models were built. During 1981 (with government approval) a Mark II version was produced; but as Dennis Poore pointed out, further development was restricted by finance and at least £1,000,000 of capital was needed if the project was to succeed.

Eventually, after a number of well publicised delays, the Mark II went into limited production as the Interpol II. In 1981 and 1982 several police forces had tried the machines and were suitably impressed. The styling of the machine had been cleverly designed to match that of the faired police BMW machines so that it blended in with the rest of the fleet when on parade and did not look unusual on the street. Orders for the machines grew during 1983 with over 130 machines bought by a number of the police forces throughout the country. Additional machines were requested by the Navy, the RAF and the Army. The Royal Automobile Club also bought a number of machines for use by their motorcycle patrols.

A civilian version of the Interpol II machine was promised to meet the numerous requests from the public, but the prospect of launching such an unconventional machine on the market was initially considered to be too risky. But the situation changed in 1984 when Dennis Poore managed to use MBH funding to buy out the £2.4 million interest held by the Department of Trade and Industry. The company was now free to seek investment from new sources and was able to expand its applications of the engine. The DTI had put limitations on the company, restricting them to the production of motorcycles and leisure vehicles only. The lifting of this restriction allowed the granting of a manufacturing licence to a major American aviation company, Teledyne Continental Motors (Aircraft Production Division) to produce both single and twin rotor Wankel engines for use in the rapidly expanding light aircraft industry. An exclusive rights licence for ten years was signed in February 1984.

For the purposes of consolidation, in 1985 MBH put NVT Ltd into voluntary liquidation. A share exchange or cash alternative was offered to the 13,000 ordinary shareholders by the new shell company, Norton Villiers Triumph Group (NVTG).

In 1987, the company was taken over by a group of investors headed by Philippe Le Roux, who became Chief Executive of the concern which was renamed the Norton Group PLC. The company had been bought primarily for its property assets, but these did not amount to the value originally predicted. In addition, Philippe Le Roux realised that the Norton name meant nothing without the motorcycle business.

So on February 27, 1987, NVTG made an agreement with BSA Limited to acquire the share and loan capitals of Norton, in addition to all intellectual property rights related to its business activities, plus the factory and office premises at Shenstone, for the sum of £1,640,000.

One of the first decisions that the new chief made was to agree to the production of the long-awaited civilian version of the Interpol II rotary machine, the Classic.

Built to test the market, the 100 bikes sold out within the first few weeks of release.

With such a positive response to the Classic, things looked good for future sales of a water-cooled version of the Norton rotary engine. This was first released as a para-military machine for the police market where it quickly found favour. Machines were also sold to the Ministry of Defence, the RAC as rapid response units, the BBC, and various other users. A civilian model was released soon after to compete with the new BMW sector of the sports touring market.

In 1987 a Norton rotary engine was used by Norton development engineer Brian Crighton in a race machine which first appeared at Darley Moor. Ridden by Malcom Heath, it went on to win a number of races which led to further development of an official factory rotary racer. The following year the factory team consisted of three riders, Malcom Heath, Trevor Nation and Simon Buckmaster. During the season they won a number of races and set new lap records at various circuits, creating plenty of public interest in the rotary machines. When Simon Buckmaster left the team just before the Power Bike International race at Brands Hatch, a new rider, Steve Spray, was brought in to take his place. He won both the Power Bike International race and the final round of the Formula One series. This impressive display attracted the attention of prospective sponsors, Imperial Tobacco, who had sponsored the Norton race team back in the 1970s. They agreed to sponsor the Norton race team for an initial period of three years.

At the start of the 1989 season, the John Player Special Norton race machines, ridden by Trevor Nation and Steve Spray, made a dramatic debut in their distinctive black and gold livery. The season turned out to be a good one for newcomer Steve Spray, but his partner Trevor Nation had a less successful time. It became clear that the team needed a professional race team manager; and that work needed to be done on the suspension of these extremely powerful machines. For 1990 the race team was headed by Barry Symmons, the former race team manager of Honda UK. He brought with him race technician Chris Mehew and suspension expert Ron Williams. From the very beginning Barry Symmons set out to organise the team into a more integrated unit, with specific tasks for each team member. This inevitably led to a clash of personalities with Brian Crighton who had his own ideas about the rotary and he decided to leave to apply his knowledge elsewhere (see p. 98).

With the launch of the reformed JPS Norton race team the company also released its superbike for the road, the sensational F1. 'The Norton F1 is the Porsche of the motorcycle world,' said Philippe Le Roux. 'It is a superb example of British innovation and technology and will take the Norton name into the 1990s as one of the most prestigious names in motorcycling.'

Civilian version of the Interpol II, the Classic.

At present the Norton group have four areas of operations:

1 The rotary engine business, which consists of research and development work on the rotary under contract and engine manufacture and sale.
2 The rotary motorcycle business; Norton is a small-volume manufacturer of hand-built performance rotary-engined motorcycles.
3 A subsidiary concerned with racing rotary powered motorcycles. The team is sponsored once more by the Imperial Tobacco group under the John Player Special banner.
4 The spares business which is a continuing and profitable concern that provides spares for the large number of Commandos still in use and the growing number of rotary-powered machines.

Despite the problems of an antiquated factory, a frequent lack of finance and a production run that in comparison with some of the other manufacturers of the time was risible (and certainly limited in its range of models) the Norton marque survived. Undoubtedly, the fame of the Norton name lies in its racing heritage of the past, and now of the present with the rotary engine. For such a small company this is a major success. Others with greater resources have tried and failed.

In racing, the future promises even greater glory now that the FIM has adjudged the rotary eligible for entry into Grand Prix motorcycle racing. Development success has come in other areas where the potential uses of the rotary engine are only just being realised. Norton rotary engines will be – and are – powering light aircraft, drones, portable generators and pumps and potentially a new generation of cars. The applications are so many that the Norton name, despite the awful uncertainties of the deepening recession in 1991, still seems a good bet to celebrate its centenary in 1998.

Development of the Wankel engine

The development of the Wankel rotary engine

The reciprocating internal combustion engine has been around for over one hundred years, and millions of man-hours and inestimable sums of money have been invested in developing and refining the basic principle. Whether they are two-stroke, four-stroke or diesel engines their basic configuration remains the same. But the Wankel internal combustion engine has only been under development since the late 1950s.

The principles of rotary engines can actually be traced back to the late sixteenth century. Around 1588 an Italian water engineer, named Ramelli, invented the first rotary type water pump. Instead of a piston, he used a single vane rotating in a housing. During the following years, he carried out further experiments and refined the first model. Since then, many different versions of Ramelli's rotary vane machines have been built, in some cases, the system has been more or less re-invented. At the beginning of this century for example, a German engineer, Wittig, designed a similar machine that incorporated a multi-vane, rather than a single vane. His version evolved into the configuration for compressors or blowers.

The English inventor James Watt produced a rotary-type steam engine in 1759. Other inventors and scientists who have carried out work on the rotary engine have included Sir Isaac Newton, Hygens and Parsons. The work done by James Watt was further refined at a much later date by Cooley, who in 1901 invented a prototype rotary steam engine in which both the inner and outer rotors rotated. This engine was further advanced by Frederick Umpleby in England in the 1960s, who attempted to apply the basic principles of planetary-type rotation to an internal combustion engine; an idea that was taken up later by the Renault company. In the 1920s and 1930s a great deal of work on the theory of the rotary engine was carried out in France by Sensaud de Lavou. In 1943, Maillard invented a rotary compressor, applying the rotary principles, from which several experimental aero-engine compressors were made. But none of these rotational motion engines had been fully developed into practical motive power units to challenge the dominant reciprocating piston type engine, until the arrival of the German engineer Dr Felix Wankel.

Dr E H Felix Wankel was born in the village of Lahr in the Black Forest area of southern Germany in 1902. From an early age he showed a great interest in mechanical things such as locomotives and aeroplanes. Felix told the story that during the summer of 1919, at the age of seventeen, he had a dream in which one Sunday morning he had driven to a concert. He told a group of friends admiring his car that it was powered by an engine that was a cross between a normal reciprocating piston engine and a turbine. The strange part of the dream was that at that age Felix had decided that he wanted to be an engineer specialising in engine design; but he had no idea of the differences between a reciprocating piston-type engine and a turbine.

He began his working life as a bookseller in Heidelberg, but in his spare time he began experiments connected with rotary types of engine. By 1924, at the age of 22, he decided that he had developed sufficient knowledge to set up and run his own small engineering workshop. During his research work Wankel had studied the theory and looked at many examples of rotary engines and realised that he could develop a rotary-type internal combustion engine with no moving parts engaged in reciprocal movement. There were a number of major problems that would need to be addressed: effective gas sealing of the combustion chamber; an efficient intake and exhaust system so that the engine could breathe efficiently; and suitable cooling and lubrication. With his own engineering facilities at his disposal it was not long before he had invented his own rotary-type engine. Granted a patent in 1929, the engine proved to be less than successful. Wankel decided that the failure of his first attempt was largely due to the inefficiency of the seals and for a rotary engine to be successful, efficient gas sealing would be the crucial factor. Many hours of work were put in to look at both existing gas sealing methods in conventional engines and to develop a new system for application in a rotary engine. His work on gas sealing gained him much respect as a specialist in this field. Research and development work is an expensive business and outside sponsorship became necessary for Wankel to continue with his development programme. To gain access to better engineering facilities, Wankel decided to join BMW where his work concentrated on producing a compact rotary valve piston aero-engine. The experience that he gained was applied to a second rotary engine design, once again without success.

In 1936, Wankel joined the German Institute of Aviation as a qualified engineer, specialising in sealing development in combustion chambers and research on valve operation. Several years later, with financial support from the government, he founded the Research Centre of Industrial Technology based at Lindau on the shores of Lake Constance, where he developed more aero-engines which used a rotary valve mechanism.

After the Second World War Wankel was arrested and imprisoned by the French. When they released him they made a proviso that he was not to undertake any rotary research. So it was not until 1951 when he joined NSU that Wankel could actively continue his work on the rotary engine. NSU were mainly interested in the rotary engine for its light weight and compactness compared to reciprocating engines. They also wished to begin manufacturing cars. They signed a deal with Felix Wankel whereby they funded his research and also provided technical support in return for his knowledge and development work on the rotary. (The NSU factory in the post-war years was mainly concerned with producing small, economical mopeds and motorcycles.) Wankel realised that for rotary engines to be wholeheartedly accepted by the management as a viable project he needed to give a dramatic demonstration of their potential.

He therefore applied his rotary valve concept to racing motorcycles. By now his work was recognised as the 'Wankel Principle'. He developed a super charger that was applied to a modified NSU 'Quickly' machine. The machine was taken to the salt flats of Bonneville in the United States where the Wankel blower generated 45 psi of boost to the intake charge, allowing the machine to reach the amazing speed of 120 mph: not bad for a 50 cc minnow!

Following this success, the NSU management realised that the rotary engine obviously had potential and gave the go-ahead for work to begin on building the unit as a complete engine. For Wankel, his dream was coming true. There were still, of course, a number of problems that needed to be overcome. For one, true rotary motion means that the rotor housing itself has to turn around a slightly different centre from the rotor. This created a number of complexities, particularly designing access for application of coolant, the oil fuel mixture and spark plug. By 1957, Dr Felix Wankel had built and tested his first rotary engine, the DKM, a complex design in which both the rotor and the rotor housing turned.

To overcome these difficulties the design team at NSU, under the leadership of Dr Walter Froede, eventually decided that the only solution lay in 'kinematic inversion'. This meant that the housing would now stay still and that the rotor would turn and move eccentrically around the chamber. On being presented with this solution (which was not true rotary movement) Wankel was said to have been aghast, 'You have made a cart horse out of my race horse,' was one of the comments attributed to him. After further consideration, he predicted that the design would generate problems of sealing at the rotor tips.

The following year, he finalised the engine which became known as the Wankel rotary engine: a triangular rotary piston turning inside a wide-bodied figure-of-eight shaped housing. This engine was the KKM. It differed from its predecessor in that it had a fixed housing and was much simpler in construction. Exhaustive tests on this KKM250 engine were carried out during July 1959 and the results proved that here, at last, was a contender to challenge the conventional reciprocating piston engine.

A Rotary Symposium which featured a demonstration of Felix Wankel's rotary engine was held in West Germany in January 1960 by the German Engineering Association. Engineers from engine manufacturers around the world were suitably impressed by the demonstration of this new engine.

On announcement of their new engine, NSU and Wankel GmbH (Felix Wankel's newly formed research and development company) were inundated with applications from over a hundred motor manufacturers throughout the world for patent licences, technical links and for development licences, particularly from those in the automobile industry. At this point it looked as if the conventional reciprocating internal combustion engine was about to be replaced wholesale with the new Wankel rotary engine: Ford, Rolls-Royce, Mercedes-Benz and General Motors all took out licences from NSU and embarked on development programmes of their own.

In 1960 NSU achieved their long term aim of producing a car powered by a Wankel rotary engine, a research and development sports car called the Prince. This was followed several years later by the first production rotary Wankel powered family car, a rear-engined model called the NSU Spider, later followed by the Ro80.

One of the first companies to sign a deal with NSU/Wankel GmbH was the Japanese car manufacturer, Mazda Motor Corporation, who agreed a contract in July 1961. Three months later, Mazda had built their own prototype engine for a highly sophisticated research and development programme which resulted in their first rotary-powered automobile in May 1967, the Cosmo Sport. This has been followed by a number of other rotary-engined models, the most celebrated being the RX7, which first appeared in March 1978. This car is now into its second generation, a beautiful looking sports cabriolet.

The Wankel rotary engine also attracted a keen interest from Mercedes. Their development programme resulted in the C111 prototype sports car, first shown in 1969, that had a three-rotor engine producing around 280 bhp giving a top speed of over 162 mph and 0–60 in 4.9 seconds.

It is intriguing to glance down the list of those 100 or so manufacturers who applied for a Wankel engine licence. The following list indicates the big hitters.

Brunswick (Mercury Marine Division)
Comotor S A.
Curtiss-Wright Corp.
Daimler–Benz AG
F. Porsche
Fichtel & Sachs AG
Ford of Germany
Friedrich Krupp
General Motors Corporation
Johannes Grauper
Klochner-Humbolt-Deutz AG
MAN (Maschinenfabrik Augsburg Nurnberg) AG
Nissan Motor Co. Ltd
Outboard Marine Corporation
Rolls-Royce Motors Ltd
Savkel Ltd
S.P.A. Alfa Romeo
Suzuki Motors Co. Ltd
Toyo Kogyo Ltd (Mazda manufacturers)
Toyota Motor Co.
Yanmar Diesel Co.

By 1971 Felix Wankel had decided that he and his partner in Wankel GmbH and Rotary Engines GmbH, Ernest Hutzenlaub, would sell their stake in the Wankel rotary licence to the British mining and industrial group, Lonrho. The fee was rumoured to be around £12 million. The licence agreement taken up dictated not only the type but the power, end use and also the sales area for the engine produced. Most of the manufacturers (apart from General Motors) involved with Wankel rotary engines through NSU-Wankel operated an exchange of development information agreement so that each member could benefit from research results. The rights attached to these licensing warrants expired in 1983.

In addition to the many automobile manufacturers who bought rights to use the Wankel rotary were a number of motorcycle and small engine manufacturers who also recognised the advantages that the rotary engine could offer over the usual reciprocating engines. Among these were the German engine manufacturers Fichtel and Sachs, and Suzuki and Yamaha.

DKW Hercules 2000

The numbers in the Hercules Wankel 2000 name did not refer to engine capacity; they were supposed to indicate the role of the machine as the motorcycle for the 21st century. It was claimed that this was the first Wankel-powered motorcycle to go into production.

Marketed first under the DKW name, the Hercules tag came later. In fact, the machine was manufactured by the giant German Fichtel-Sachs AG company who had bought an NSU-Wankel licence back in December 1960, the terms of which stated that they could build gas engines capable of producing between five and thirty horse power. In addition to the Hercules, (classed as a touring machine) the company produced several two-stroke machines, off-road machines and a very successful 47 cc moped.

The Hercules was unusual in that instead of the conventional layout, running the engine fore and aft, the rotor was in line with the rear wheel; the engine lay across the frame. The result was a small, compact, odd-shaped engine, fronted by a large cooling fan that made the engine look like a turbine. Engine displacement was a claimed 294 cc, although it must be said that this was the capacity of one chamber. The machine received a mixed reception from the press at the time. A lot of criticism was made of the styling, the dated Italian switch gear and a poor gearbox, (later replaced). The main opinion though, was that the engine was incredibly smooth and turbine-like in its power delivery.

Van Veen

Dutch motorcycle importer Henk van Veen went his own way with his project OCR100 superbike. Taking a Moto-Guzzi frame he fitted a Mazda sports car engine and completed the rest of the machine with no expense spared.

The resulting superbike, announced in 1976, featured a twin rotor engine measured as 996 cc, with a four-speed gearbox, electric start, disc brakes front and rear. The top speed was around 130 mph despite a dry weight of 642 lb (291 kg). The heavy weight also carried a hefty price tag, in 1977 it was over £5000. The machine was an excellent piece of engineering for the very few who could afford it; but these were too few it appears, as Henk van Veen finally closed the production unit in 1978.

Yamaha

Yamaha actually built and exhibited a Wankel rotary motorcycle that featured a twin rotor engine rated at 1320 cc capacity. The engine was in fact a modified version of one that was already being produced by the Japanese Yanmar Diesel Company. Charge-cooling was used for the rotor although some of the induction air was bypassed to increase power output. After its show debut few details of its technical specifications were made available and a date for its production was never given, so one must assume that the project was shelved.

Suzuki RE5

In 1974, Suzuki were the first Japanese motorcycle manufacturer to release and put into production a rotary-powered machine, the RE5. It was rushed through design and development to ensure that they stole a march on everyone. Confidence was high in the new engine. The expensive manufacturing rights had been purchased from NSU and re-tooling for what was expected to be high numbers production had been

Mazda RX7 Turbo Cabriolet.

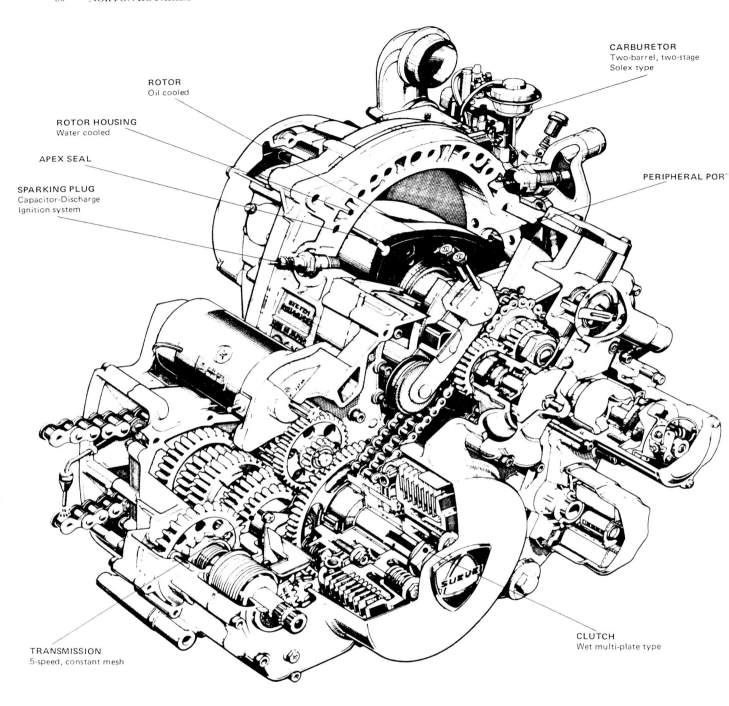

CARBURETOR
Two-barrel, two-stage
Solex type

ROTOR
Oil cooled

ROTOR HOUSING
Water cooled

APEX SEAL

SPARKING PLUG
Capacitor-Discharge
Ignition system

PERIPHERAL PORT

TRANSMISSION
5-speed, constant mesh

CLUTCH
Wet multi-plate type

Suzuki's rotary engine, licenced by NSU/Wankel.

carried out. The rotary engine was, after all, seen by many as the future for the entire industry.

The 497 cc machine was very modern in styling and its complex engine unit was tightly fitted into the frame in addition to a very large radiator with a fan behind it. Engine cooling was by water, but the single rotor was oil-cooled. It was a heavy machine and probably because of the rush into production, it suffered poor throttle response and dubious handling. It was also blighted by a heavy fuel consumption that drastically hit its sales during the oil crisis. It was withdrawn in 1977, having sold only 440 units.

Principles of operation

The Wankel rotary engine works on the Ottocycle principle, in that it has four distinct individual phases: the familiar induction, compression, expansion (this is the actual power phase) and exhaust.

The rotor turns within the housing with its three apices following and always in contact with the inner surface of the trochoid chamber (see diagram overleaf). Three separate working chambers are thus formed around the rotor within the two-lobe trochoid chamber. The Otto-cycle is completed in each chamber in turn in *one* revolution of the rotor.

This was BSA's starting point when they bought the Wankel licence (in reality a single rotor Hercules for further evaluation).

In other words, a change from maximum chamber volume can only take place after the rotor has travelled through 90°; ie when one rotor flank moves from position 1 through 2 and 3. The volume thus contained increases gradually and induction occurs. During the following 90° movement the compression, expansion and exhaust phases take turn in strict sequence. One complete thermodynamic cycle is occurring in each of the three chambers as the rotor turns through 360°. The drive shaft turns three times for one revolution of the rotor. This determines that every thermodynamic phase extends over 270° of drive shaft rotation. This relative movement is controlled by an internal ring gear that is incorporated within the rotor that in turn meshes with a stationary pinion fixed to the outer end cover.

The Norton twin rotary engine has three basic moving parts: an eccentric shaft, which also acts as the drive shaft, and two rotors which are needle-roller-bearing mounted on the eccentric shaft. They are mounted at 180° to each other to counterbalance. The eccentric, or output shaft (equivalent to the crankshaft in a reciprocating engine) is so called because the rotor

OPERATING SEQUENCE OF THE WANKEL ENGINE

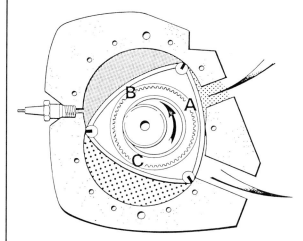

A ░░░ INDUCTION
B ▓▓▓ COMPRESSION
C ░░░ POWER STROKE

Induction of fuel/air mixture commences when the rotor achieves position A.

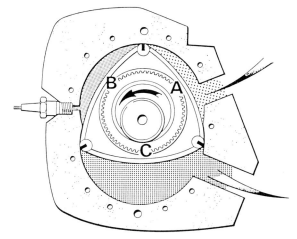

A ░░░ INDUCTION
B ▓▓▓ COMPRESSION
C ▓▓▓ EXHAUST

With continued rotation, the fuel/air mixture is compressed at position B.

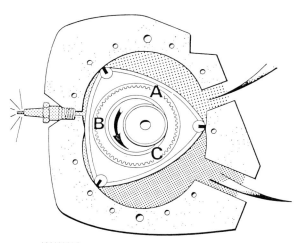

A ░░░ INDUCTION
B ▓▓▓ IGNITION
C ▓▓▓ EXHAUST

When the rotor attains position B, the compressed fuel/air mixture is ignited.

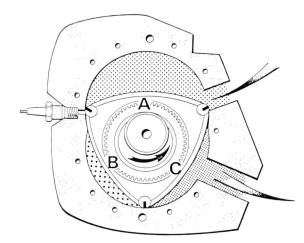

A ░░░ INDUCTION
B ░░░ POWER STROKE
C ▓▓▓ EXHAUST

The gas expands providing the power, until exhaust occurs on reaching position C.

ABOVE RIGHT Cutaway model of the rotary engine.

RIGHT Eccentric shaft.

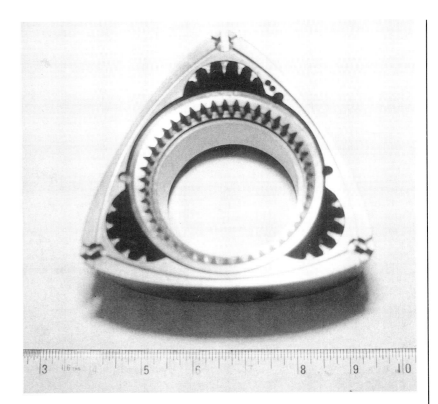

RIGHT **Rotor showing fins.**

BELOW **Rotor located on eccentric shaft, showing recesssing in rotor flank.**

OPPOSITE **The trochoidal shape of the rotor housing.**

bearing areas are offset to those of the main bearings.

The three apices and side flanks of each rotor incorporate spring-loaded gas seals that push out against the inner surface of the trochoidal combustion chamber housing. This ensures that an efficient cycle of induction, compression, expansion and exhaust is maintained.

The eccentric rotor shaft is forged in EN 36 steel and is supported at each end by substantial roller main bearings located in each stationary gear housing mounted within the aluminium end-plates. Air cooling passages are drilled axially through the shaft below the rotor needle-roller-bearings journal surfaces. The rotors themselves are cast with internal integral cooling fins in axial passages at each of the three corners of the triangular rotor.

As it passes through the centre of the engine the air not only cools the internal surfaces but also distributes the oil mist to all the moving parts before passing into the working chambers of the engine.

The basic geometry of the rotor and the meter housing is not easy to explain. A specific trochoid curve is necessary for the rotor to rotate smoothly to form its distinct working chambers. The inner surface of the rotor housing is correctly termed the 'peritrochoid curve', usually called epitrochoid, or trochoid. The shape of the trochoid is described by the path generated by a point within a circle rolling around another large circle, when the radii of the small rolling circle and the large stationary circle are in the proportion of 2:3. A two-lobe peritrochoid of the Wankel engine is thus generated.

The problem of efficient sealing of the chambers was solved when each of the seals was lightly spring loaded and the inner surface of the rotor housings was coated with Elnisil or sprayed tungsten carbide to increase the wear properties of the surfaces. (Elnisil, or Nicosil, contains minute particles of silicon carbide.)

Drive is taken from the right end of the eccentric shaft by a hydraulically-damped enclosed duplex primary chain. Power is transmitted through an all-metal multi-plate clutch to a five-speed constant mesh gearbox then via a main chain to the rear wheel.

The left end plate of the eccentric shaft carries the engine fly wheel and generator. A capacitor discharge electronic ignition unit is triggered by an inductive pickup that is mounted adjacent to the periphery of the flywheel.

BSA initial experiments

The BSA group, who were an extremely large and powerful company at that time, had also begun to show an interest in this revolutionary type of engine. As a major engineering concern, it ran a group research centre located at Kitts Green near Birmingham, an area noted for its large pool of skilled engineering workers. The Research and Development Centre was therefore

Trade stand advertising for the engine first looked at by David Lockley, the Fichtel and Sachs KM914.

one of the best facilities in the country for engineering studies to be carried out on the new engine. The Wankel programme started as a very small operation managed by development engineer David Lockley; his brief was simply to look at the new Wankel engine. (In fact what he looked at was a German Fichtel and Sachs KM914 fan cooled engine.) The job brief was then expanded to include feasibility studies for using the engine to power a motorcycle. As this venture was a definite motorcycle project, David Lockley was transferred from the Kitts Green Group Research Centre to the motorcycle division's own research and development centre at Umberslade Hall near Solihull.

A little earlier, in 1969, development engineer David Garside had joined the research staff at Kitts Green. He had been attracted by the job description that had mentioned working on a new type of engine which he had correctly interpreted as being the Wankel, on which he had already gained some experience at Rolls-Royce.

After some experimentation on different types of frame the two engineers managed to fit the Fichtel and Sachs single rotor fan-cooled engine into a BSA Starfire frame. Eventually they had a complete-machine that was extremely ugly to look at but was capable of travelling around the local countryside so that an assessment could be made of its performance.

The results from the initial trials proved to be sufficiently encouraging for the project to continue. Having carefully monitored and reviewed progress on the project, David Garside had already decided that in his opinion the Wankel engine was more suitable for applications in large capacity, high-performance motorcycles. In smaller units, its initial high production costs and relatively high fuel consumption militated against successful manufacture or marketing. The decision to build a larger air-cooled engine using twin

rotors was frowned upon by Fichtel and Sachs. They were considered to be the world experts on the air-cooled Wankel engine at the time. In their opinion, the cooling problems would be insurmountable for a large, high-powered, air-cooled installation. Fichtel and Sachs were basing their assessment upon their experiences of developing small single rotor engines for use in many applications, such as generators. These engines were often run flat out for long periods of time, which meant they generated massive amounts of heat. So they believed that if David Garside actually produced a twin rotor, high performance engine it would run at such high temperatures that it would cause rapid engine failure. It was not too long before Fichtel and Sachs actually produced a large capacity Wankel powered motorcycle themselves, the Hercules 2000. This amounted to a challenge to David Garside, who had a keen interest in thermodynamics, engine cooling and heat dissipation and who believed that he could produce an engine that would be sufficiently cooled to operate successfully.

David Garside believed that he could design an engine that would require neither fan or water cooling. His research into the best method of engine cooling took more than twelve months to complete and involved reading every piece of information he could find on engine cooling using fins to dissipate heat. This research soon showed that in theory the new Triumph triples, with their triple bank of cylinders with only the minimal cooling fins would soon overheat. According to research, the cooling fins were insufficient in depth to dissipate the heat sufficiently. In reality though, the Triumphs soon proved themselves more than capable of high performance under racing conditions, where engine temperatures would obviously be very high. David Garside therefore concluded that engine temperature was dependent upon the way the engine was used and the air flow over and around it; if the design was right, he would need no other form of cooling.

The Fichtel and Sachs KM914 had a charge-cooled engine; this means that the incoming fuel, oil and air mixture is drawn through the centre of the rotor thereby cooling it before it enters the chamber. Further cooling was achieved by forced-air cooling of the housings or conventional finning. The chamber capacity was nominally measured as 300 cc with a power output of around 18 bhp.

The first reaction was that the power output from what could be generally regarded as the equivalent to a 600 cc reciprocating engine was disappointing. But despite the low power output it was felt that the mechanical simplicity of this charge-cooled engine was attractive when compared to the complexity of the oil-cooled rotor type.

Efficient cooling of any engine is essential to prevent damage to the internal mechanical parts: seizure due to heat expansion, excessive engine wear from burnt oil or pre-ignition of the incoming charge into the chamber are three major problems. For reference, engine cooling efficiency tests on the KM914 were carried out to find heat rejection rates, optimum cooling surface areas, etc. A number of tests were also carried out on the track to evaluate the maximum and minimum available cooling air flow velocity over the engine whilst a motorcycle was moving. The data thus obtained indicated that a single

rotor engine such as the KM914 could not be adequately cooled in all operating conditions without a supplementary cooling mechanism such as a fan.

Additional experiments on determining the cooling available and the cooling actually required were carried out on both two-stroke and four-stroke reciprocating air-cooled motorcycle engines. The results showed that when most of them were operated at or near peak power they were not adequately cooled theoretically, yet they all continued to perform despite peaking into excessive temperature zones.

The idea of using water-cooling for a motorcycle engine was considered but quickly rejected as unacceptable in the motorcycle market at the time. It wasn't until the arrival of the Suzuki GT750 water-cooled 750 cc two stroke in 1971 that water cooling was considered to be marketable. With hindsight, the resistance to water cooling is surprising, considering the number of water-cooled machines around now.

Measurements on some of the BSA motorcycle engines showed that these only had 20 in²/bhp of cooling because they were located in an area receiving air at only half the velocity of the machines forward speed. Obviously, the front wheel created an area of slower moving air behind it and the cooling efficiency was greatly decreased.

The base model for the experiments, the KM914, had a cooling fin area of 50 in²/bhp, operating a single rotor. It was believed that a twin rotor version of this

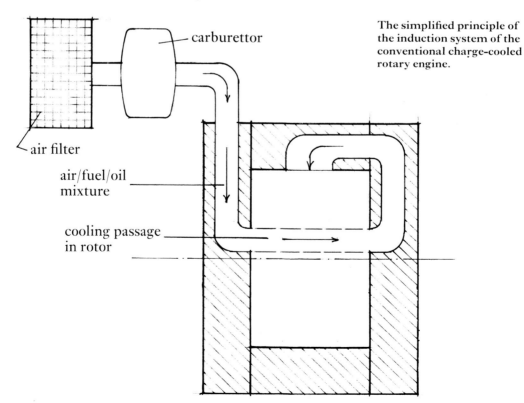

carburettor

air filter

air/fuel/oil mixture

cooling passage in rotor

The simplified principle of the induction system of the conventional charge-cooled rotary engine.

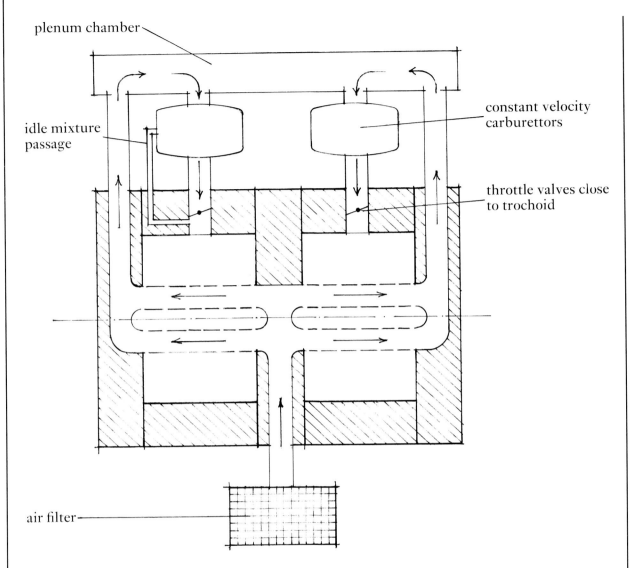

plenum chamber

constant velocity carburettors

idle mixture passage

throttle valves close to trochoid

air filter

engine would be more applicable for motorcycle use as the increased housing fin area would provide more efficient cooling. To further improve air cooling, the engine needed to be located as low as possible in the motorcycle with the rotor housings exposed as much as possible to free air undisturbed by the front wheel.

Cooling was further improved by tilting the engine 15° to the rear, thereby exposing the area of the housing between the spark plug and the hot lobe major axis, where major heat generation occurs. Circumferential finning also ensured an even spread of heat across the trochoid chamber thereby preventing heat distortion.

With the engine in this position, the inlet pipe could be routed over the top of the transverse gearbox with the exhaust down pipes passing underneath. Using the information gained from their experiments, the development team designed and built a twin rotor engine with the same internal dimensions and moving parts as

the Fichtel and Sachs KM914 engine, for further work on increasing power.

Thus in the spring of 1970 the first twin rotor engine with air and charge cooling was completed and fitted into a BSA A75 Bandit frame. People didn't like the look of the 38 bhp engine this prototype, the R2. They said it looked like a motorcycle driven by an electric motor. Despite the comments on its appearance the machine performed extremely well in providing smooth power delivery. The project team felt that they were on the right track.

All the work being invested in the Wankel project, now located at the BSA Group's Motorcycle Development and Testing facilities at Umberslade Hall was taking place against a background of BSA's continuing financial difficulties and on more than one occasion the design team was reduced to David Garside alone.

Despite the mechanical simplicity of construction in

the charge-cooled rotor engine there are several draw-backs to this system. Firstly, the incoming charge is heated as it passes through the rotor which results in a low maximum BMEP (Brake Mean Effective Power, a measure of engine efficiency). Secondly, the long inlet path through the rotor restricts engine breathing at high speeds.

Various designs were tried using a partial bypass system in which only a proportion of the induction air was drawn through the rotor, the rest passing directly to the working chamber. The resulting marginal power increase was offset by the reduction in rotor cooling in a system where the KM914 had already shown signs of being close to the limits.

Attention then focused on alternative means of induction. In one BSA experiment, the heated mixture emerging from the rotor was ducted through an air-to-water intercooler before passing into the induction chamber. Work was carried out on the openings in the housing end plates. The original half-lemon shape opening was eventually expanded to a full lemon shape. With this system there was less restriction on the incoming charge.

The unsatisfactory intercooler was replaced with a plenum chamber of five-litre capacity, allowing expansion and subsequent cooling of the incoming charge. A major breakthrough in increasing power output came from repositioning the carburettor between the plenum chamber and the induction chamber, so that only air passed through the rotor and not the mixture. Using this system with a single rotor engine gave an amazing 85% more power when compared to the original KM914 engine output.

LEFT **Revised induction system with air only passing through the rotors.**

BELOW **Lemon-shaped opening in the side housing.**

So by the spring of 1971 a solution to the cooling problem had been found. David Garside decided that by careful positioning of very deep fins around the housing, no fan would be needed. Obviously a twin rotor housing would provide a greater surface area for the location of cooling fins.

The essential breakthrough had been the drawing of air only through the rotors and not the air-fuel mixture as in the original engine. This allowed the temperature of the fuel charge mixture to be lowered from 100°C to 50°C before entering the combustion chamber. The total temperature drop was partly achieved by passing the air through the plenum chamber, a large volumetric chamber allowing expansion and therefore cooling of the air. The temperature dropped from 100 to 75°C in the chamber, and the further 25°C reduction was obtained by the evaporation of the fuel in the carburettor. The charge density was subsequently increased, which therefore created a greater power output. The slight drawback of this revised induction system was that the plenum chamber had a capacity of five litres which made it rather bulky (though it also helped reduce induction noise).

David Garside and his development team concluded that this significant rise in power output was entirely due to the improvements they had made to the increase of volumetric efficiency during induction.

There were three main reasons for the improvement:

1 The opening up of the end plate to a full lemon shape meant that the incoming charge was less restricted and therefore lost little of its velocity and with the wider area at any angular position of the shaft, at least two paths were open through the rotor.
2 The plenum chamber reduced the charge's temperature as it expanded. The chamber also helped modify the highly intermittent working chamber intake flow to a steadier flow through the restrictive rotor and side-plate passages. More effective use was made of the passages to reduce pressure loss, especially important for a twin rotor engine having a single plenum chamber.
3 The revised position of the carburettor allowed the latent heat of fuel evaporation to be utilised more favourably, giving a lower final mixture temperature.

Fine tuning of induction was achieved just as it is with a two stroke: namely, working on the length and the diameter of the inlet pipe between the carburettor and the inlet port. However, a drawback to the system was that by routing air only through the rotor, engine lubrication now required a separate oil metering pump and oil reservoir tank. A fuel oil pre-mix system like that of a two-stroke engine, in which oil is mixed with the petrol in the tank at refuelling was rejected as unsuitable for the envisaged high-quality motorcycle that was the aim of the development project. Subsequently, a system that fed a small amount of oil into the inlet tract below the air filter was used.

But would the new system of induction adversely affect the operating temperature of the rotor? Like a two-stroke cylinder, one lobe of the rotary chamber, where expansion and exhaust take place, runs much hotter than the other where induction and compression are occurring. The rotor itself during its four cycles (like the piston crown in a reciprocating engine) does not therefore expose the rotor flanks to such high temperatures as the trochoid housing lobes. In fact, the total quantity of heat received is usually less than 10% of that being given off by the igniting mixture to the main outer housings. A small amount of the heat generated during operation is lost by conduction from the rotor via the gas side seals to the main side housings. But sufficient further cooling must be achieved in order to prevent the gas seals from sticking and to provide a satisfactory working temperature for the rotor bearing. The cooling ability of the induction air volume is sufficient for this, depending upon the outer housing temperatures being kept low by finning or some other method.

The induction air rotor cooling system gives a near automatic balance of cooling under most load and speed conditions. Further increases in power output and the resulting heat input to the rotor is simultaneously balanced by a corresponding increase in air volume flow internally. Under no condition is the rotor over-cooled. Low rotor temperatures lead to higher fuel consumption and hydrocarbon emissions, both unacceptable consequences these days.

Any weakening of the mixture necessary for optimum fuel economy does not cause rotor overheating, because greater heat input is offset by an increase in airflow. This is because the induction cooling air is used more effectively when passed through several passages in parallel more slowly and constantly, rather than through one passage at high velocity and intermittently.

The lower final charge temperature reduces the gas temperatures throughout the cycle and therefore reduces the heat input through the rotor flank. At maximum load, this more or less cancels out the adverse effect of the induction air only – and not the total mass and lower temperature fuel/air mixture – being passed through the rotor. At part-open throttle, there is an added advantage that the cooling medium in the rotor passages is now at ambient pressure. Prior to the change of the carburettor position, the cooling medium was at the throttled inlet pipe pressure and was therefore composed of reduced density gas. For a vehicle application, when overrun with a completely closed throttle occurs frequently, this is an important factor. Overall, the alternative approach of using a special oil cooling system for the rotor was much less attractive because of the associated cost, space, leakage, and wear problems.

Despite all the difficulties and the pressures that he was placed under, David Garside continued to persevere with the Wankel development. Many times he

actually designed parts of the engine, built them, tested them and if necessary rebuilt them, himself. Surprisingly, despite all the cutbacks that were made to save the firm from collapsing no-one ever thought of cancelling the Wankel development project. At one point, when things did appear to be very close to disaster, David Garside actually suggested that instead of being paid redundancy money he would rather come to some arrangement by which he could acquire the engines he had built, along with all drawings, patterns and technical information he had collected on them.

Eventually BSA became absorbed into the Norton-Villiers-Triumph group NVT headed by Dennis Poore, who had an engineering background and was able to recognise the potential of the Wankel rotary project for himself. Despite the concern about the company's financial difficulties and no doubt after reasoned argument from David Garside, Dennis Poore allowed the project to continue. The premises at Umberslade Hall had been disposed of, and so the project returned to the Research and Development Unit at Kitts Green.

Much of the time after this early research work was completed was spent in development of the concepts outlined, to obtain reliability and durability, together with further increases in power output and reduced fuel consumption. Two development machines were built using a sheet metal chassis to assist in research.

The press were desperate for information on the machine and it was fairly common to see photographers lurking in the bushes opposite the factory hoping to get a picture of one of the prototypes. Eventually they had the opportunity to test ride a machine. The report by *Motor Cycle Weekly* in April 1975 trumpeted the prototype as 'the world's most desirable motorcycle'.

Cool Heads and Idle Hands . . .

In August 1975 the NVT Group of companies went into liquidation, as described in Chapter One. Dennis Poore was keen for the Rotary research to continue, and moved the project to a small factory at Lynn Lane, Shenstone, not far from Lichfield in Staffordshire. Here a small team under Bob Trigg set about designing the final machine based around the sheet metal monocoque frame that housed the oil tank and the plenum chamber.

Several prototype motorcycles were built with twin rotor 600 cc engines. These were road tested, much of this work being carried out by Bob Rowley. Bob's early impression of the machine was that it was incredibly smooth and quick, though its pull start was comical.

'The first ride was not uneventful, we were doing some carburation work and due to the weather conditions the inlet tract froze the throttle wide open. As it was a prototype there was no ignition cut-out so I was going round the track wondering whether to lay this

One of the twin rotor prototypes test ridden by John Nutting in the summer of 1974. (EMAP)

valuable prototype down before I eventually managed to switch the fuel off. David Garside who had been watching promised me that it was nothing to worry about, that it couldn't happen again.' (Some time later Bob took David Garside, who is not a motorcyclist, on the back and took great delight in subjecting his passenger to a number of scares; it is rumoured that David Garside has never been back on a bike.)

During these test riding sessions the riders would cover long distances, often venturing into Wales or wherever their fancy took them. Bob Rowley recalls, 'I remember stopping for a call of nature once and propping the bike up against a nearby black and white post, I had been so eager to ride that I couldn't wait for the fitters to put a side stand on. I did not realise that the post was plastic and I suddenly saw that it was bending and I could do nothing about it as the bike landed on top of me in the ditch. On returning to the factory I was not flavour of the month.'

Development work on the engine was still being carried out to ensure reliability and also keep it competitive with the rest of the motorcycle market. Attention was focused on the rotors, specifically the recess shapes and depth in the rotor face, to improve combustion. Various tests were carried out on both leading and trailing shapes with associated changes of location of the spark plug. The leading shape proved to be the most successful providing up to 10% increase in torque and improved fuel consumption. However, the original F&S design rotors, which has been satisfactorily road tested to 60,000 miles without failure, cracked after only 5,000 miles with the new design. This problem was compounded when more power was needed from the engine. Early experiments included screwing plates to the rotor flanks to increase the compression ratio. The prototype machines with these modifications were known to the test riders as the hand grenade rotaries, as they tended to blow up if the screws holding the plates sheared off under the high combustion pressures. These machines were even faster than those running today, as they were not restricted by the requirements of silencers.

The solution to these problems was found in the new design of the rotor: its gear teeth were cut as an extension of the steel outer race. The new design also incorporated cooling fins in the rotor corner passages which helped to lower the temperature of the bearing outer race and the rotor.

David Garside

David Garside could rightly be called the father of the Norton rotary engine. It was his work and dedication that coaxed and forced the engine into production for its many applications. He was born in Yorkshire the second son of a farmer. He won a place to study Mathematics at Emmanuel College, Cambridge but then decided after his first year that he wanted to follow a mechanical engineering course. Whilst at university, David was fascinated by a model engine that was located in the entrance hall to one of the schools: a perspex model of the then new Wankel engine. The model actually worked, so that interested students could turn a knob that caused the rotor to follow all its phases of induction, compression, ignition and exhaust. David achieved a first class honours degree in Mechanical Sciences and won the prize for the best technical paper in Thermodynamics. He left Cambridge to join Rolls-Royce Motor Car Division as a graduate apprentice; within ten weeks or so of his arrival he was working on the development of the chassis and suspension of the Rolls-Royce Silver Shadow.

After serving his apprenticeship he left Rolls-Royce to work for the Central Electricity Generating Board, but kept in touch with his former colleagues. 18 months after leaving Rolls-Royce, David was persuaded by one of his friends to go back to work on the diesel rotary engine programme that was starting at this time. He built up valuable experience of the rotary concept whilst on the programme. He eventually left to become chief engineer with a small company making agricultural machinery at Devizes in Wiltshire, a sort of return to his farming background.

It was then that he saw a job advertised at the BSA motorcycle company to work on the development of a new type of engine. The advertisement did not mention the rotary engine, but he was pretty sure that this was what they were planning to develop. He got the job: 'I suppose I was probably the only person who did apply for the job who had had some experience of the Wankel rotary engine.'

At this time BSA was a large and successful company with a number of different divisions. David went to work at their Kitts Green Group Research and Development Centre near Birmingham. Here he had a test bed for setting up and running test engines and was supported by a staff of three. The motorcycle division who were actually funding the research work into the rotary engine decided that for them to keep greater control over the work the project should be moved to their own research and development centre at Umberslade Hall, Hockley Heath near Solihull.

Development work on the rotary engine was progressing well when it became apparent that the financial difficulties that had hit the British motorcycle industry as a whole were beginning to affect BSA. One of the first assets to be wound up was the Research and Development Centre. Despite the winding down, he and ten other engineers – there had been over 200 engineers based there before – continued their work on the project for another 12 months. Eventually with the formation of the Norton Triumph group, funding was made available for the project to return to Kitts Green as part of Norton Triumph International Ltd, the marketing and engineering arm of the group. With the eventual collapse of the companies, at least 90% of the projects were closed down. David Garside managed to persuade Dennis Poore who was head of the group that the rotary project should continue. So in 1976 David moved again, this time to the Shenstone factory, near Lichfield, where he has carried out most of his development work since.

As Director of Engineering David was responsible for the development of the rotary engine that eventually powered the Interpol II. His work was also focused on refining and testing the engine for marine and aviation use. For the past few years he has been mainly concerned with these two applications. In 1982 he delivered a technical paper to the Society for Automotive Engineering in the United States on the development of the Norton rotary motorcycle engine.

Cracking began to develop around the spark plug hole as the power increased and the solution suggested was to replace the material of the housing with a higher hot strenth alloy. Even copper inserts were tried, but the answer was not to be found until water cooling was adopted.

The low copper content of the higher hot strength alloy also aided bonding with the Elnisil coating of the trochoid bore to reduce wear. This nickel-silicon coating provides a very durable surface which is compatible with the IKA3 cast-iron rotor apex seals.

Another difficulty facing David Garside was how to achieve a satisfactory idle quality, comparable to a reciprocating engine. Because of the late closing of the exhaust port, exhaust gases mix with the incoming charge. At idle, only a small charge is required and this is obviously liable to greater dilution. The solution lay in restricting the idle mixture to one rotor, which caused a parastic drag from the non-firing rotor. The additional load caused a larger fresh charge to be drawn in. By using this system it was now possible to achieve a steady 850 rpm idle speed with no misfire.

A total loss lubrication system had been adopted at a very early stage of development but occasional smoking from the exhaust led to the fitting of small bore drain tubes, feeding into a pocket at the bottom of the induction air transfer passages in each end plate and also to the base of the plenum chamber. These tubes were then connected to the main inlet pipes located between the carburettors and the throttle valves. When the throttle was opened the additional vacuum created by the hydraulically dampened carburettor piston drew the oil into the incoming charge to be burnt during combustion.

Meanwhile prototype test riding was continuing. One night returning from a run in Wales, Bob Rowley, who does not hang around on a motorcycle, noticed that he was being followed by a police motorcyclist so he dropped his speed but was stopped. The policeman began by admonishing Bob for his speed but then started looking at the machine. When he found out that it was a Norton rotary he wanted to know all about it. He then intimated that a test ride of his own might ensure that justice was blind re the speeding! As Bob recalls, 'I happily agreed to this and seconds later he went screaming off into the dark; a couple of minutes later he came wailing past me and disappeared. I began to feel unsure and made a hasty check of his machine which, fortunately, was a police machine. With its radio chattering away, I was pretty safe. He came back twenty minutes later, thoroughly pleased with himself. He had obviously ridden the bike hard as the rotor was clicking and clacking away because of expansion.'

Only Bob Rowley and Fred Swift were supposed to ride the prototype machine and so Bob wisely reported what had happened to his boss Tony Denniss, Director of Motorcycles. The following day there was a fire at a

Doug Hele

Doug Hele obtained an HNC from Birmingham Central Technical College and served his apprenticeship with Austin Motors from 1935 to 1945. He became Design Draughtsman with Douglas (Kingswood) Bristol until 1947. He then joined Norton as assistant designer to Bert Hopwood. He developed the Norton Lowboy and Dominator racing machines and assisted in the design of the Jubilee and Navigator twins. Invited to join Triumph at Meriden by Hopwood, he was in charge of the Daytona racing shop and worked on the BSA/Triumph triples and the 350 Bandit that never went into production. Doug became Designer and Chief Development Engineer at Norton, BSA and Triumph, a post he held until 1975. He then left the motorcycle industry to work on marine engines with British Seagull outboard engines at Poole, where he was Chief Designer and Technical Director, but returned to work with David Garside at Norton on the Wankel project in 1982 as Chief Motorcycle Development Engineer. He is still designing at Norton at the time of writing at the age of 71!

Doug is a member of the Motor Industries Executive Club. The club meets twice a year for long weekends. The one stipulation for attending these weekends is that you ride a motorcycle. Doug rides a 'stripped down rotary which looks more like a Classic' and does 150 to 160 miles a day over the weekend, depending on the venue.

Tony Denniss

Tony Denniss, B.Eng. M.I. Mech E. London Technical College, HNC, ONC, has worked for Norton for over thirty years. He was working for Associated Motor Company as chief draughtsman and then as chief designer when AMC took over Norton, and was responsible for the transfer of the production of the Commandos from Plumstead to Wolverhampton in 1969. From 1969 to 1978, he was special project engineer and travelled Europe and the States procuring motorcycle components. He was largely responsible for the development of the very successful range of Commando motorcycles. With the development of the rotary engine, he helped produce the Interpol II Police motorcycle. In 1979 he became General Manager at Shenstone, promoted to Director of Motorcycles in 1984. When he retired in 1987 he did not disappear from the scene but made himself available for work on special projects.

He owns several motorcycles – a Commando, a Matchless G12 GSR and a Triumph 250 Tigress (but confesses to being a fair weather rider).

Bob Rowley

Bob Rowley has over 25 years experience in the motorcycle industry, firstly (and I suspect more enjoyably) as a test rider and secondly in charge of quality control. He first began training with BSA, where he became a development engineer specialising in high speed and endurance test riding.

He worked as a test rider for Norton through the 1970s. He was involved in the high mileage road testing which took place on the rotary prototypes and on the testing of bikes at MIRA. He was lucky enough to take the first rotary racing prototype round MIRA (after Dave Evans had tried it out in the factory yard!). Bob moved into Quality control at the beginning of the 1980s and is now Chief Inspector with overall responsibilities for motorcycle testing.

chemical factory just down the road and everyone had to leave the Norton factory. Bob happened to be in a car with Tony Denniss. They were stopped at a road block manned by the same policeman. Seeing the Norton badge on Tony's jacket, he mentioned his little adventure of the previous night! Bob must have been very relieved that he had informed Tony of his misdemeanour the night before.

By the end of the 1970s there was reasonable certainty of technical success. The design of a completely new, fully styled production motorcycle could start. At this time Bob Trigg left the project and Tony Denniss transferred from his post as Special Projects Engineer to replace him. In the same year 25 MkI production prototypes had been produced. The following year (despite Dennis Poore's concern about the need for capital investment) a number of MkII machines were built and loaned out to various police forces for testing. These machines were the fore-runners of the Interpol II.

The Interpol II

With the successful development of a twin rotor air cooled engine, the go-ahead was given for the design of what was to become the Interpol II motorcycle. This machine was specifically for police and service use and many unique features were incorporated into its design. The project was carried out by a development team that included Tony Denniss and then at a later date Doug Hele. In 1982 the latter rejoined the compny with the specific brief of refining and developing David Garside's ideas using his vast wealth of practical experience. When further power development resulted in occasional rotor shaft bearing failure, it was Doug Hele who came up with the solution. The original system had oil entering the engine and travelling out to the rotor bearings, by which time it had lost some of its lubricating qualities. Doug Hele decided to reverse the air flow so that it passed first through filters and then to the end plates where it collected the lubricating oil to carry it to the rotor bearings. Another problem he tackled was the tendency to 'snatch' that was found with the Interpol II when subjected to long periods at slow speeds whilst on traffic patrol duty. The cause of this 'snatch' was the transition from single rotor firing whilst idling to twin-rotor firing engagement under normal load. Doug Hele reverted to a twin-rotor idling system with a built-in ignition retard system controlled by speed and temperature.

In addition to its development of the air-cooled engine the project team also carried out simultaneous development of a water-cooled engine. By the end of 1979 the team had produced 25 Mk I production prototype air-cooled machines. Despite satisfactory road test reports the machine did not go into production, partly because of government reservations about the potential sales of the machine, (it will be remembered that the Department of Trade and Industry had a controlling stake in NVT at this time). The project continued nevertheless, and construction of a number of Mk II production prototype machines began in the early months of 1981.

To fully test these prototype machines Norton approached the traffic departments of interested police forces around the country who could then be loaned machines with the option of buying. As part of the deal, information on the performance of the machines would of course be supplied back to Norton for appraisal.

The major attraction to potential buyers from this market was the lightweight, (around 100 lb), very powerful engine that required little routine servicing and gave a very high mileage. Norton's confidence in the power unit was demonstrated by their offer of a three-year unlimited mileage warranty on the engine. The majority of other manufacturers only offered a 12-month warranty period and their machines required regular servicing approximately every 3000 miles. A major concern for a fleet operator is the reliability and service intervals of any machine that is in use. The Interpol II rotary engine only required a service after covering around 6000 miles.

More than 20 police forces took up the option and during 1981 and 1982 reports on the machine's performance in police use began to come back. Overall, the reports were very favourable but a number of consistent criticisms began to emerge, such as problems with tick-over, rotor seals blowing and over-heating. Most of these problems were exposed as a direct result of the characteristics of police traffic patrol riding, having to ride at slow speeds for long periods of time. Under these conditions the engine was subjected to massive heat build-up that had adverse effects on its performance.

To rectify the tick-over problem, the project team first altered the electronic ignition system and then made changes to the carburation that successfully smoothed engine idle speed down to an impressive 600 rpm. Most large capacity motorcycle engines idle at around 1,000 rpm, or even higher, to achieve a smooth tick-over.

The problem of engine over-heating was then addressed: and many eyes turned once again to the water-cooled engine. Despite these problems over 140 Interpol II machines had been delivered to around 30 of the police forces around the country during 1983; a further 20 machines were supplied to the Ministry of Defence for use by the Royal Navy and the Royal Air Force, and the Royal Automobile Club also purchased a number of machines. This growth in production led to an increase in the workforce at Shenstone and the opening of a service workshop to maintain the machines.

Interpol II Engine

The engine featured a 'Total Loss' lubrication system like a two stroke which meant that there is no need for

oil or filter changes. Oil is taken from a tank formed within the frame of the machine and fed to the engine in metered amounts governed by a combination of engine speed and throttle opening. An oil/air mist is formed when the oil is distributed from the metering pump via two feed pipes to each side of the aluminium alloy intermediate plate and meets the incoming charge of cooling air.

After the oil mist has carried out its task of lubricating the eccentric shaft, rotor gears and the bearings in the housings it is burnt during combustion. Evidence of this action can be seen when the machine is started from cold or during tick-over when a slight exhaust haze can be emitted, just like a two-stroke engine.

The cool air that is drawn into the engine via the air filter then passes through the intermediate plate where it mixes with the oil from the metering pump to form a fine lubricating mist. This is drawn through the rotor and the cooling passages in the shaft to openings in the left and right end plates, then up through the hollow forward engine mounts and into the plenum chamber contained within the frame. By passing through the centre of the engine the air cools the internal surfaces and also distributes the oil mist to all the moving parts of the engine before it passes into the working chambers of the engine and is burnt.

The fuel/air mixture is provided by two S.U. HIF 4 constant depression carburettors that draw air from the plenum chamber. The throttle butterflies are fitted directly in the inlet ports of the combustion housing. On later machines with twin rotor idle facility, an additional auxiliary flywheel auto advance ignition system was used that incorporated in both inlet ports an auxiliary fuel-air mixture feed pipe, running directly from each carburettor and bypassing the throttle butterfly. It thereby adjusts idle control on both combustion chambers.

On the earlier machines (prior to engine number 3110) single-rotor idling was used where the left inlet port was fed from a throttle-operated, solenoid-controlled valve allowing through unfuelled air directly from the plenum chamber when the throttle was in the closed position. This action is known as single rotor idling and causes the left rotor to stop giving power, which increases the drag on the right rotor and therefore makes for a stable idle quality. This is achieved without additional flywheel inertia or the electronic ignition retard facility.

Drive power is taken from the right side of the eccentric shaft by hydraulically damped, enclosed duplex primary chain that transmits the power through an all-metal multi-plate clutch to the gearbox. The left

Inspecting the first Interpol II are (left to right) Denis Austin, Dennis Poore, Prince Michael of Kent, Tony Denniss and Roy Ward.

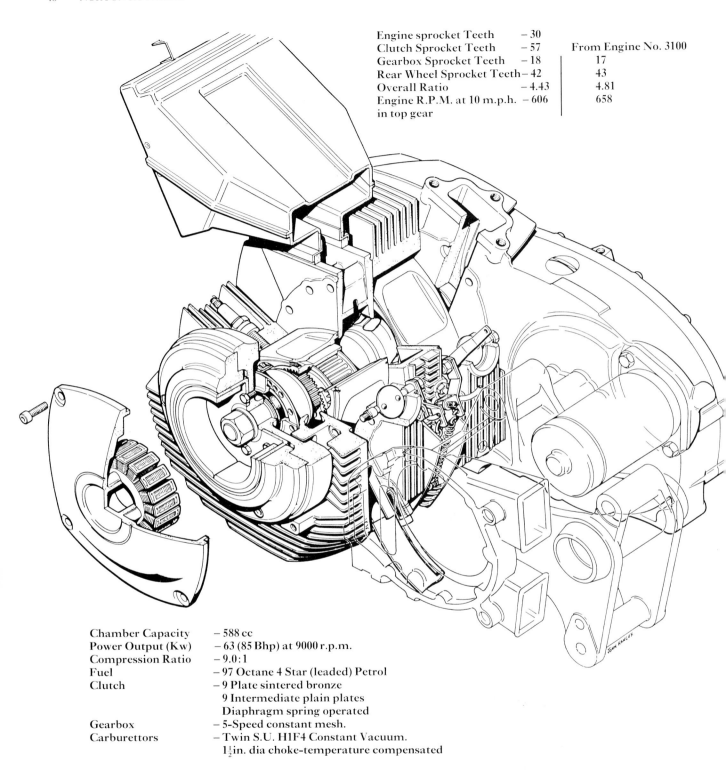

Engine sprocket Teeth	– 30	From Engine No. 3100
Clutch Sprocket Teeth	– 57	
Gearbox Sprocket Teeth	– 18	17
Rear Wheel Sprocket Teeth	– 42	43
Overall Ratio	– 4.43	4.81
Engine R.P.M. at 10 m.p.h.	– 606	658
in top gear		

Chamber Capacity	– 588 cc
Power Output (Kw)	– 63 (85 Bhp) at 9000 r.p.m.
Compression Ratio	– 9.0:1
Fuel	– 97 Octane 4 Star (leaded) Petrol
Clutch	– 9 Plate sintered bronze
	9 Intermediate plain plates
	Diaphragm spring operated
Gearbox	– 5-Speed constant mesh.
Carburettors	– Twin S.U. H1F4 Constant Vacuum.
	$1\frac{1}{2}$in. dia choke-temperature compensated

Twin chamber rotary engine as fitted to the Norton
Interpol II Police Motorcycle.

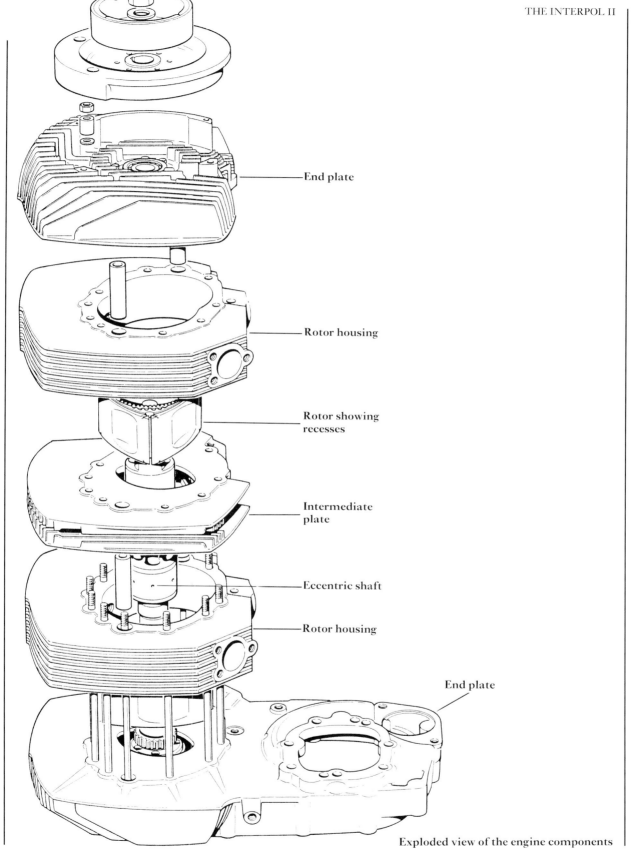

End plate

Rotor housing

Rotor showing recesses

Intermediate plate

Eccentric shaft

Rotor housing

End plate

Exploded view of the engine components

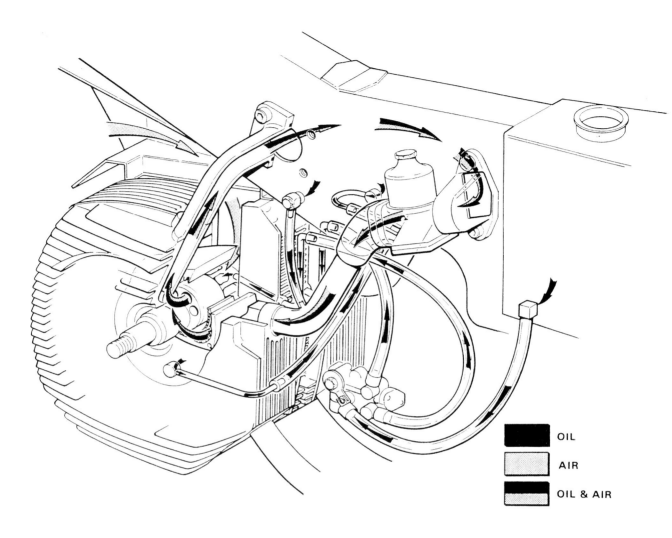

	OIL
	AIR
	OIL & AIR

Engine lubrication system.

end of the shaft carries the engine flywheel and generator. A CDI or Capacitor Discharge Electronic ignition system is triggered by an inductive pick-up mounted next to the outside edge of the flywheel.

The twin triangular rotors are mounted on needle-roller bearings at 180° to each other on the forged eccentric shaft. Each rotor is cast with internal integral cooling fins in axial passages in each of the three angles of the rotor. The eccentric shaft incorporates cooling air ducts horizontally bored through the shaft and the shaft itself is supported at each end by roller main bearings. These are mounted in each stationary gear housing located within the aluminium end plates.

Ignition is governed by an electronic system giving reliable performance without the need for adjustment. The unit is an electronic capacitor discharge coil ignition system that comprised a variable reluctance electro-magnetic pulse generator. This is usually refer-red to as an 'Ignition Trigger Unit'. The ignition

trigger unit and electronic ignition unit were designed specifically for this machine and are not replaceable with components from other sources. The specified unit incorporates an engine revolution limiter that operates at 9250 plus or minus 150 rpm, which prevents damage to the rotors from over-revving. The ignition trigger unit initiates the required pulse when a step in the flywheel crosses the pole piece of the trigger unit. It is located between the flywheel and the left engine end plate, behind the flywheel/generator cover. On single-rotor idle machines, the trigger unit and air by-pass micro-switch are, on each side of the end plate.

The capacitor discharge ignition system is located under the left electrical side cover which is removed by releasing the 'Dzus' fasteners at the front of the panel. The spark plugs are Champion 10 mm surface discharge type which have a platinum centre electrode and are designed to be partially self-cleaning. The appearance of the spark plug, usually a good indicator of correct combustion operation, does not provide a positive indication of mixture strength. Service life is normally in the region of 15000+ miles, when plugs should be replaced as there is no means of adjustment. The charging system of this machine is a Kokusan alternator that feeds a 12 volt 14 amp/hour battery via a specifically designed electronically controlled voltage regulator.

The gear box is a five-speed constant mesh unit with an eighteen plate metal clutch assembly that provided light positive action combined with maximum durability, all features looked for by fleet operators such as the police or armed services.

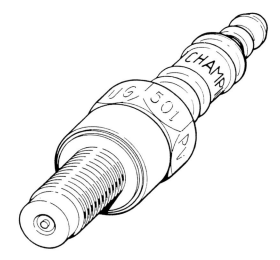

ABOVE **Surface discharge type spark plug.**

BELOW **Diagram of 5-speed gearbox.**

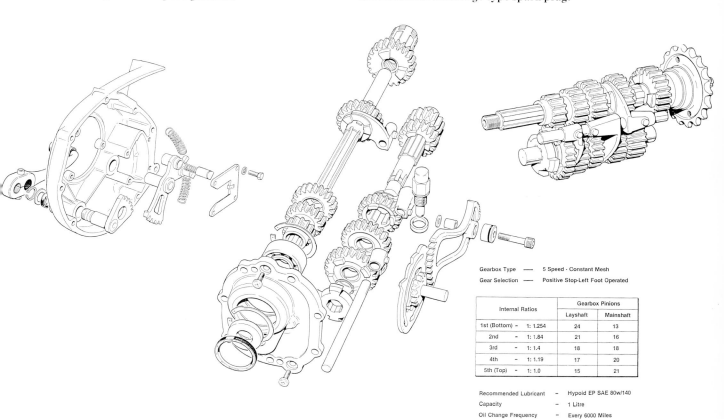

Gearbox Type —— 5 Speed - Constant Mesh

Gear Selection —— Positive Stop-Left Foot Operated

Internal Ratios		Gearbox Pinions	
		Layshaft	Mainshaft
1st (Bottom) -	1: 1.254	24	13
2nd -	1: 1.84	21	16
3rd -	1: 1.4	18	18
4th -	1: 1.19	17	20
5th (Top) -	1: 1.0	15	21

Recommended Lubricant - Hypoid EP SAE 80w/140

Capacity - 1 Litre

Oil Change Frequency - Every 6000 Miles

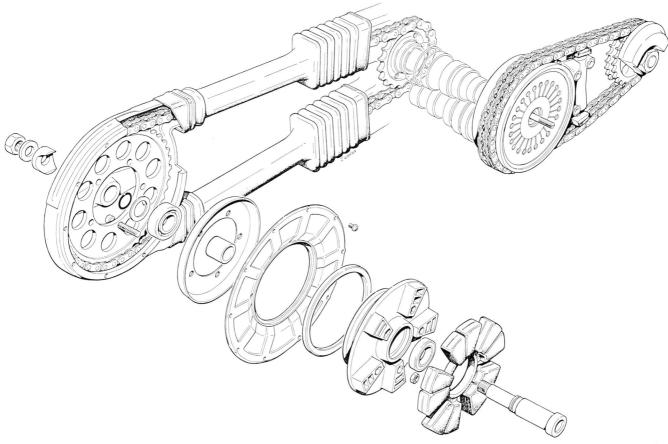

Transmission and Suspension

The engine unit transmits power by sprocket and duplex primary chain to the clutch chainwheel housing that contains the multi-plate all-metal diaphragm spring clutch. From the clutch, power is transmitted through the gear box to the high gear and gearbox final drive rear chain which runs in an enclosed oil bath to the rear wheel sprocket. The rear chain specified for this machine is a single row $5/8 \times 3/8$-in 112-link Renold 'Grand Prix'. Running this in an oil bath prolongs its life to around 80,000 miles and reduces the need for chain adjustment.

Unfortunately, it was felt that there was not a suitable British manufacturer able to supply the front suspension units, wheels or brakes and so approaches were made by Tony Denniss to Italian firms who were highly regarded at this time for their suspension work. Development work was successfully undertaken by Norton with leading Italian firms to produce the high standards that Norton required.

Suspension and Frame

The rear suspension is controlled by two matched Girling gas-assisted spring and hydraulic damper units.

ABOVE **Diagram of transmission system. The clutch embodies a five vane rubber-segment-filled shock absorber.**

RIGHT **Diagram of front forks.**

The suspension unit consists of a sealed gas hydraulic damper unit and outer coiled spring for pre-load adjustment to three levels, to vary ride height and handling requirements.

The front suspension is of telescopic design. The lower sliders are made from aluminium alloy sliding on chrome-plated steel stanchion tubes with internal coiled suspension springs. To aid servicing the forks can be drained in situ at specified intervals by means of a drain plug on each sliding member and oil replenished through the easily accessible top plug assembly.

The frame is an extremely rigid basic spine to which the engine is directly attached, made from 16 swg sheet steel in box section. The plenum chamber was formed in the front section of the frame with the centre part containing a four-litre engine oil reservoir and the rear section forming the mud guard and an exceptionally

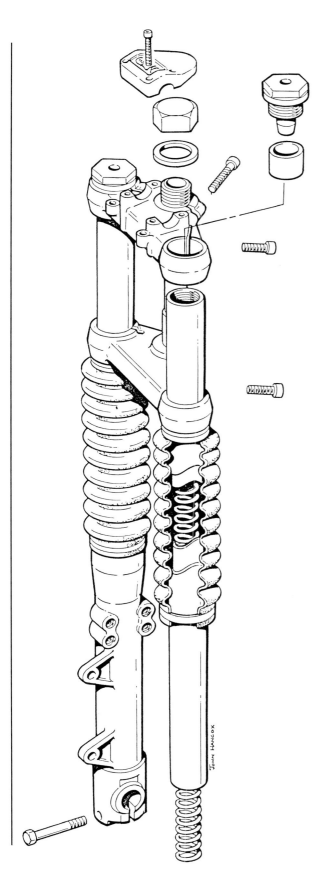

strong mounting point for the rear suspension units, radio pack, panniers, etc. The frame itself was zinc phosphate coated primed, then powder-coated to provide durable corrosion resistance undersealed under the rear suspension. The rigid design construction provided a good strength-to-weight ratio which, combined with the high performance suspension, helped high-speed stability and handling characteristics.

Wheels and Brakes

The brakes on this machine are 'Brembo' disc brakes, twin units on the front, single unit on the rear. As they are self-compensating for wear, no adjustment of the brake system is possible apart from minor adjustments of the rear brake pedal height. The aluminium rear brake pedal pad is detachable so that it can be relocated into one of four alternative positions to suit the individual rider. Each caliper has a pair of pistons fitted with 'Textar' all-weather sintered bronze brake pads for maximum efficiency in all weather.

Both the front and rear wheels were of cast alloy construction and were fitted with high performance 'V' rated Pirelli 'Phantom' tyres. Both wheels are quickly detachable. To ensure accurate relocation of the rear wheel, calibrated wheel adjusters are used.

Considerable thought went into the design of a full fairing, (for a machine that would be operating in most weather conditions), to keep the rider protected from bad weather and wind buffeting. To reduce servicing time, the bottom panels were quickly detachable.

Standard equipment included two tone siren, daytime driving lamps, a quartz clock, a 23-litre (5 Imperial gallons) fuel tank with automatic vacuum-operated petrol tap, rear fog guard lamps, hazard warning lights, an illuminated Police stop sign, an electronic tachometer, 140 mph-calibrated and certified speedometer, forward-facing flashing blue lamps, convex spring-mounted and fully adjustable rear view mirrors.

The company was also able to offer a wide range of optional equipment which included a wailer siren, front and rear strobe lights, a single rear strobe light on a telescopic mast, a 'Whitehall' radio fitting kit and a built-in battery charger. Other equipment within reason could also be fitted upon request. Each machine was delivered ready for use and only required the tuning of the radio, (Norton were the only manufacturer allowed to fit government radios), number plate and road fund licence.

Tony Denniss Safety Motorcycle

In September 1987 Tony Denniss, who had been largely responsible for the development and success of the Commando range of machines plus the Interpol II, retired as Director of Motorcycles at Shenstone. But he was still around for special projects.

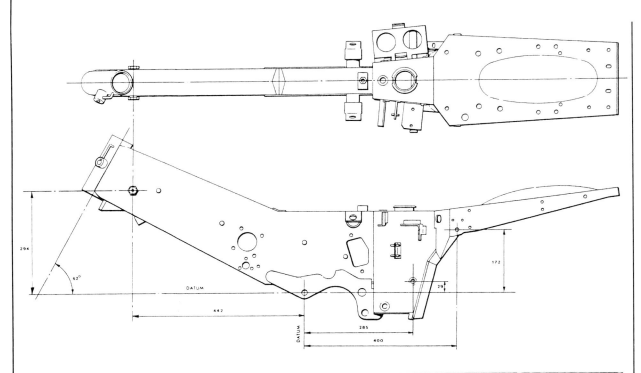

One of the projects he had been working on previously had been a special exercise to develop a safety motorcycle for the Transport Road Research Laboratory. Usually, the TRRL made their safety machines themselves and this was the first time that they had approached a manufacturer to produce a safety motorcycle for them. The machine that he helped to develop, over a 14-month period, featured a number of safety devices such as a tank-borne impact-activated air bag to protect the rider in case of accident, a safety cage and special fairing to lessen impact, minimising damage to rider or machine. There were energy absorption cells for leg protection, the revolutionary introduction of Lucas-Girling Anti-lock brakes, an anti-spill petrol tank that included a fuel supply cut-out if the machine went over on its side and high intensity running lights. The machine made its debut at the International Technical Conference on Experimental Safety Vehicles in the United States, where it was so well received that Tony Denniss was awarded the United States Government's National Highway Transport and Safety Administration Award for 'Engineering Excellence' for his prototype safety motorcycle.

ABOVE LEFT Diagram of frame, plenum chamber formed in the front section.

LEFT Interpol II with police equipment. The mounting point on the frame for the rear suspension units, panniers and radio had to be unusually strong.

RIGHT Tony Denniss' safety motorcycle, with energy-absorption cells for leg protection, amongst other safety features.

Other Applications

Light Aircraft

The BSA research group at Kitts Green produced a brochure in the early summer of 1970 entitled, 'A proposed 100 bhp Air-cooled Wankel engine for Light Aircraft' which aroused great interest in the light aircraft manufacturers.

One small light aircraft manufacturer had already begun to use a Wankel Fichtel and Sachs KM914 rotary engine to experiment. After only 200 hours total flying time, (the Air Registration Board had only granted flying permission one day at a time), they had discovered that cooling was not a problem. In fact, work on re-directing the heat generated was needed to avoid icing of the carburettor in the temperatures found at higher altitudes. To comply with regulations they had to use a twin pole spark plug with two separate ignition circuits, and propeller speed needed to be between 2,000 to 3,000 rpm which would require the engine to be geared down from its 6,000 rpm running speed to about 2.3:1 for maximum efficiency. Having met the research team and discussed their findings they were keen to work with BSA on developing and using the engine. But for this to happen, government funding would be required. Approaches would therefore need to be made to the National Research and Development Council (NRDC) and to the Ministry of Technology; and BSA would acquire an NSU/Wankel licence.

The performance characteristics of the proposed twin rotor engine based upon the Fichtel and Sachs KM914 engine were given as:

Total swept volume	600 cc
Maximum power output	48 bhp at 5,500 rpm
Maximum torque	46 lb. ft at 4,000 rpm
Specific fuel consumption	0.62 lb/bhp hr
Oil consumption	2% of fuel flow
Weight	74 lb

With their commitment to continued development, Norton can now offer a choice of designs and manufactured gasoline-fuelled Wankel type rotary, lightweight engines, capable of producing between 20 and 120 bhp (15 to 90 kw). These engines all meet with Civil Aviation Authority standards and are suitable for a wide range of applications. With the development of new composite materials and Norton's production of light

but powerful engines it is hoped that the combination will result in less expensive aircraft that will expand the total market.

This could open up three promising areas for rotary sales, in the large United States market for new aircraft, in the expanding European market, and in the aircraft engine refit market. Aircraft engines need to be overhauled after every 2,000 hours; Norton rotary engines, once they have been granted type certification, will be able to offer operators the opportunity to replace their existing engines with rotaries promising better performance, and lower weight, and at a price that is competitive with the cost of an engine overhaul. Work is currently taking place under licence with the major United States aviation company, Teledyne Continental Motors (Aircraft Production Division). The company will make the Norton rotary engine in versions for both military and civilian use, to sell on.

The cost of these engines would be very competitive when compared to other aero engines. An endurance testing and flight trials programme is in progress and the engineering programme aimed at flight certification will continue through the 1990s.

Interest in the use of rotary engines has come from other sectors of the burgeoning light aircraft industry, where the engine could be used in motor-gliders, auto-gyros, microlights and home-built aircraft.

The NR642 engine comprises a heavy duty version of the basic twin rotor engine that is integrated with a dedicated helical-spur reduction gearbox with a high prop line. The rotors are air-cooled by a belt-driven centrifugal fan, although it is possible to use the exhaust ejector system when noise is not a critical factor. The housings themselves are water-cooled. The engine is designed to meet the British Civil Aviation regulations, its European equivalent and the United States Federal Aviation Authority certification standards, US certification was expected during 1991. The engine was approved by the CAA in December 1990 for use in civilian passenger aircraft.

Part of the CAA regulations for aircraft engines require that the engine is run at full power for a minimum of 150 hours non-stop! At Norton in the test and development section the engines are run at 8,000 rpm and full power for 150 hours then the engine is removed from the test rig and stripped for inspection. The engine is then re-assembled with the same parts

and seals and run for a further 150 hours. This is the equivalent of running the engine on the road for a distance of over thirty five thousand miles at a constant speed of 120 miles per hour without stopping.

1989 saw the installation and first flight of the NR642 in the Shaw 'TwinEze' light aircraft and also in the Australian-made Seabird Sentinel. The Norton NR642 light aircraft engine made its maiden public flight at the Popular Flying Association rally at Cranfield on July 1. Two of the 90-hp engines were installed in the revolutionary Twineze by its builder Ivan Shaw. The Twineze which cruises at around 175 knots, uses three bladed propellors with a 53-in diameter mounted on its rotary engines, acting as pusher-type engines mounted on the wing trailing edge. Ivan Shaw is the

TOP **The NR 642 powers a Seabird Sentinel.**

ABOVE **Ivan Shaw's 'Twineze' canard-type aircraft.**

General Manager of Aviation Composites Ltd, a company specialising in the design and manufacture of aircraft built entirely from advanced composite materials. The company is in fact a former branch of the Lotus car company.

After the flight Ivan Shaw commented, 'I am delighted with the performance of the Norton rotary engines in my aircraft. The rate of climb is excellent and

NR 642 - GF - 90

ROTARY AEROENGINE FOR LIGHT AIRCRAFT

The NR642 aeroengine has been designed and is being developed to meet UK CAA/European JAR-E certification standard. It is anticipated that it will also be certificated to the equivalent US FAA FAR-33 certification standard.

DESIGN FEATURES

Exceptionally high power to weight ratio.
Small frontal area.
Economical fuel consumption.
Integral reduction gearbox (allowing efficient and quiet propeller speeds).
Low levels of vibration.
Suitable for either tractor or pusher installation.

TECHNICAL SPECIFICATION

Type	Wankel-type rotary, spark ignition engine.
Displacement	Twin rotor - 294cc per rotor.
Power	90 bhp at 7,000 engine rpm (standard 20°C, 760mm day).
Weight	142lbs (65kg) for full wet running installed assembly. Dry weight as illustrated = 124lbs.
Housing Cooling	Water - glycol mixture with integral centrifugal pump and dual thermostat system.
Rotor Cooling	Air-cooling using belt driven centrifugal fan.
Direction of Rotation	Clockwise (looking at face of prop flange).
Ignition System	Fully duplicated C.D. system with magnetic triggering. R.F. shielded.
Carburettors	Twin Tillotson diaphragm type. Close-in mounting ensures no carb icing. Altitude mixture compensating device under development.
Fuel Feed	By gravity or 12v electric pump plus pressure-pulse diaphragm pump.
Fuel Type	Avgas (100LL) or Regular grade (min 92 RON) automotive leaded gasoline.
Specific Fuel Consumption	0.50lb/bhp hr at 70% cruise = 4.3 Imp gallon/hr (Avgas) = 5.2 US gallon/hr
Lubrication	Total loss via metering pump from separate tank.
Oil Usage	2½% of fuel flow.
Oil Type	Castrol A545 (synthetic) or Mobil Pegasus 485 or equivalents.
Starting System	Electric 0.6 bhp 12v starter motor.
Generator	26 Amp/12 volt (brushless, flywheel mounted). Vee-belt driven, high output/28 volt options to be available.
Propellor Flange	SAE.1 specification.
Gearbox	Integrated helical gear reduction gearbox including anti-torsional vibration device (external rubber) with high prop line. Standard ratio 2.96. Alternative gear ratios of 2.47 and 2.03 are available.
Vacuum Pump	Optional belt-driven pump with standard AND 2000 mounting pad. Sigma Tek IU28A pump can be supplied as extra.

NOTE

Certain design features of the engine are covered by British, US and other foreign patents.

LEFT Specifications for the NR 642-GF-90 engine.

RIGHT According to Ivan Shaw, the Norton engine is well suited for light aircraft application, smooth and powerful.

the engines are as smooth as turbines. it sounds like a Spitfire! I started the installation programme after meeting with Norton last autumn. The hard work to design the twin engine configuration and mount the two engines is now bearing fruit.'

The reaction from David Garside, Norton's Director of Engineering was just as enthusiastic: 'I have always felt that the rotary engine had its greatest potential in light aircraft. The low weight and smoothness are key advantages. The rotary will enable major advances to be made in light aircraft design. We have already completed the Civil Aviation Authority's JAR-22 test, the regulation under which aircraft engines are certified safe for civilian use. We now aim to achieve a full Certificate of Airworthiness from the CAA and the FAA for passenger-carrying aircraft. The inaugural flight marks an important milestone in this work.'

The TwinEze aircraft has been adapted by Ivan Shaw from the original Rutan-designed, single-engine 'Longeze' canard-type aircraft. Norton have also engaged Rogers Aviation of Cranfield to fit an NR642 rotary engine into a Cessna 152 for flight trials during 1990.

The NR622 engine has a similar core to the 642 engine but uses a lighter gearbox with a low prop line. The rotors are induction air-cooled and the housings are water-cooled. This engine produces 82 bhp in power output and is considered to be most suitable for application in ultra lights, autogyros, and light aircraft. The latest model of this engine, the P62, uses an exhaust ejector system of rotor cooling which further increases its power output to 90 bhp.

The NR642 is similar to the NR622 but it does not have a reduction gearbox. Its applications could include light aircraft and helicopters with in-built reduction drive. A high-performance version using an exhaust ejector system for rotor cooling can give up to 120 bhp which makes the engine suitable for racing boats and hovercraft.

Defence Applications

A second major market for Norton has been the growth in demand for unmanned aircraft: military drones and Remotely Piloted Vehicles, RPVs, assisted by the development of new materials and electronic miniaturisation.

RPVs are mainly used for surveillance, reconnaissance, (including battle zone assessment, as they were in the Gulf War) and weather observation. Traditionally RPVs have been high speed machines powered by very expensive turbo-jet engines. With decreasing defence budgets the change has been to new generation lightweight 30 to 150 bhp reciprocating engines. The well-known superior power-to-weight ratio of the Norton rotary engine and its low vibration and noise levels

MODEL NR801

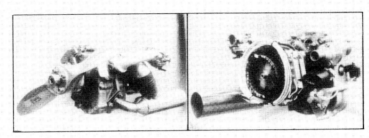

NR801-DE-40 ROTARY AEROENGINE FOR DRONES & RPVs.

The NR801 is a highly optimised, light-weight, single rotor, liquid cooled engine. It has an integral mounting of a 0.9 to 1.5 kW, 28 volt brush-less and bearing-less generator.
It has been designed and developed specifically for existing and future drones and RPVs.

DESIGN FEATURES

Exceptionally high power to weight ratio.
Small frontal area.
Low levels of vibration.
Economical fuel consumption.
Suitable for either tractor or pusher installation.
Direct-drive propellor.
(An optional lightweight reduction gearbox may be available in the future).

TECHNICAL SPECIFICATION

Type	Wankel-type rotary, spark ignition engine.
Displacement	Single rotor – 294cc per rotor.
Power	40 bhp at 6,000 engine rpm. Alternatively up to 60 bhp at 8,000 engine rpm (standard 20°C, 760mm day)
Weight	Basic engine weight as illustrated is 43lb (19.5kg) Fully installed weight with cooling system generator is 53.7lb (24.4kg)
Housing Cooling	Water-glycol mixture with tooth-belt driven pump.
Rotor Cooling	Air-cooling using exhaust ejector system.
Direction of Rotation	Anti-clockwise (looking at face of prop flange).
Ignition System	Electronic CD system with magnetic triggering. R.F. shielded. Duplicated system firing twin spark plugs is available as option.
Carburettor	Diaphragm-type.
Fuel Feed	By pressure-pulse diaphragm pump.
Fuel Type	Regular grade (min 92 RON) automotive gasoline (with or without lead)
Specific Fuel Consumption	0.50lb/bhp hr at 70% cruise = typically 2.0 Imp gallon/hr (2.5.0 US) 0.56lb/bhp hr at maximum.
Lubrication	Total loss via metering pump from separate tank.
Oil Usage	224cc/hour at 6,000 rpm.
Oil Type	Castrol A545 (synthetic)
Starting System	Via external cranking at propellor hub.
Generator	900 watts/28 volt Plessey direct mounted at rear of main shaft (weight is 9.9lb-4.5kg). Alternative winding gives 1.5kW.
Gearbox	Optional integral straight spur gear reduction gearbox (3.00:1; 2.50:1 and 2.00:1 is available) including anti-torsional vibration device (internal mechanical coupling) with low prop line.
Vibration	Nominally zero (± 20cm gm) radial imbalance. Peak-to-mean torque fluctuation is 4 approx.
Exhaust System	Exhaust ejector only.
Mounting	Platform or bulkhead mounting via 4 x M8 bolts.

NOTE

Certain design features of the engine are covered by British, U.S. and other foreign patents.

when compared to the reciprocating engines obviously make it attractive in this sector of the defence market.

Drones are used for target practice in military training exercises and Norton have been busy in promoting the performance and price characteristics of its engines to drone manufacturers worldwide. In short, the rotary engine offers a high power-to-weight ratio similar to a two stroke engine, but the fuel consumption for the same distance is much lower. When compared to a four stroke the fuel consumption is similar, but the weight of the engine is much lower. Therefore the rotary engine would make possible the use of larger and faster craft than those powered by reciprocating engines. The time in the air of these craft should also improve by as much as 20 to 25%. So a rotary powered drone or RPV is capable of longer missions or of carrying a greater payload than one powered by a two stroke or four stroke reciprocating engine.

In addition radial vibrations are eliminated and torsional vibration is at a very low level, this reduces the stress placed on the airframe and also has advantages for the sensitive electronics which may constitute the payload. Rotary engines are not highly stressed and have long life and low maintenance requirements, all bonuses to military budgets. During 1989 the NR642 engine was chosen by the joint McDonnell Douglas/Developmental Sciences Corporation team as the best power plant for use in the United States Department of Defence's short range RPV.

The Norton NR801 is a single rotor engine with liquid cooled housings and no reduction gearbox and it has been designed and developed specifically to give a compact and lightweight unit for RPVs. Rotor cooling is with an exhaust ejector.

Another single rotor engine is the NR731 which features ram-air-cooled housings and rotor; this model has the highest power-to-weight ratio ever achieved by a production rotary engine. It has been designed specifically for use with military target drones. And is currently used for powering the Target Technology Banshee 300, an RPV that is manufactured in the United Kingdom, amongst others.

Norton also manufacture and service the small KM48 engine which is used as a power generator for the mobile radar units manufactured by Thorn EMI Electronics Limited. These small but very robust units are widely used by the armed forces throughout the world and are considered to be superior to conventional engines in their ability to withstand the abuse they receive in the field.

LEFT **NR801-DE-40 specifications: note the fuel consumption and vibration claim.**

BELOW **Norton NR731 in Banshee 300.**

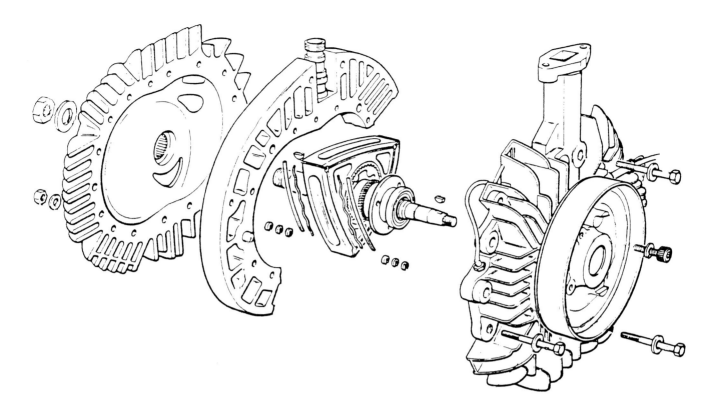

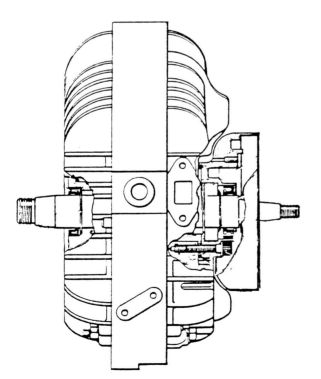

OPPOSITE, ABOVE **Engine module KM48**

THIS PAGE **Exploded view of the extremely robust KM48 engine module, as used to power mobile radar units** (RIGHT) **designed by Thorn EMI Electronics Limited, units such as the Cymbeline used by British Forces are well able to withstand a battering in the field and have a tolerance to low-quality fuel.**

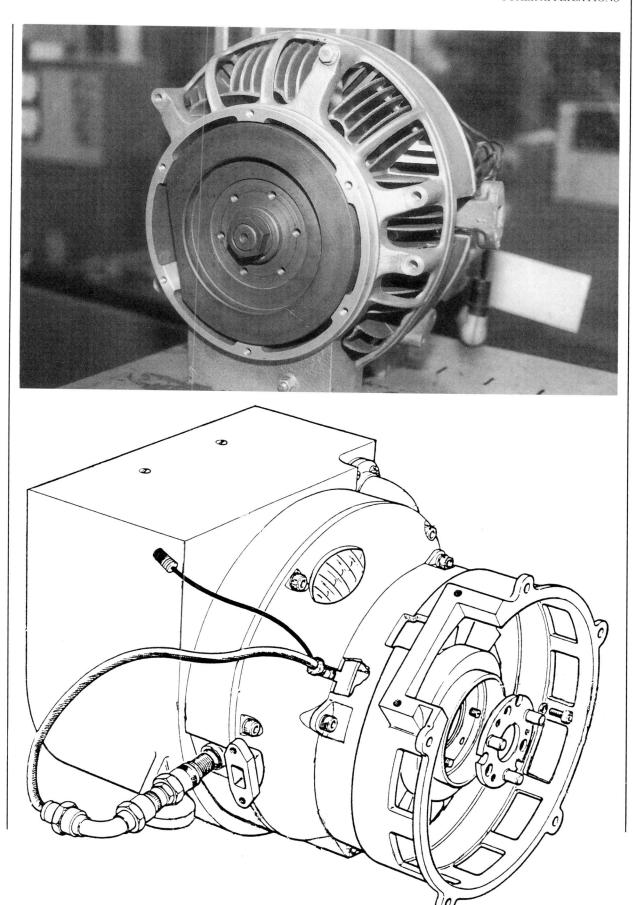

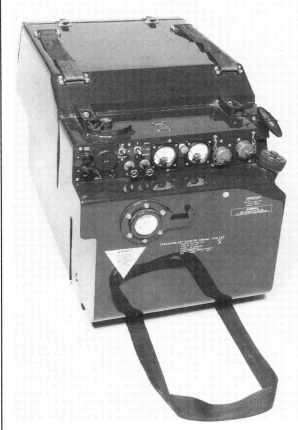

ABOVE **Ground power generator for Thorn-EMI Cymbeline radar.**

RIGHT **Hovercraft fitted with two different rotary engines, one for thrust and one for lift.**

Automobiles

By 1981, Dennis Poore felt that a water-cooled variant of the engine was more acceptable as even more power was necessary to be competitive and he also felt that it might be interesting to fit an engine into a car chassis. To encourage efforts in this direction he arranged for an Austin Metro car to be delivered to Shenstone with instructions that it was to be fitted with a water-cooled engine as soon as possible. This obviously put David Garside and the development team under greater pressure; when Mr Poore next visited the factory, (which he did every fortnight) he was asked which should take priority. He replied that the motorcycle should take first priority but shortly after inquired when the car would be ready for him to test drive.

Becoming impatient, Dennis Poore turned to one of his subsidiary companies, Carbodies, who also made London taxis and asked them to install the engine. When completed the vehicle was returned to Shenstone for development and occasional test drives by Dennis Poore, who happened to be a former racing driver. By 1983 Dennis Poore was finally happy with the performance of the car and decided to satisfy the curiosity shown by Austin Rover with a demonstration of its ability. The demonstration certainly had an effect on the development personnel from Austin Rover who were dismayed to find that the rotary-powered car easily out-accelerated their MG Metro Turbo! When Austin Metro showed no further interest in the car Dennis Poore decided to use it himself. He gradually felt that he wanted even more performance. To satisfy his need he pressed David Garside into fitting two water-cooled engines bolted together in-line, producing 87 bhp each into a Reliant Scimitar SS1. The performance was stunning, according to the few brave passengers who experienced a drive in this monster machine, too powerful for the Ford Cortina clutch and rear axle to cope with.

There have been several other experiments fitting Norton rotary engines into car bodies but no specific project has since been carried out because this was too divorced from the company's core development programme.

Hovercraft

As time passes, more and more people are finding that the Norton rotary engine makes a superior replacement to normal reciprocating engines in a variety of applications. Bill Yates from Cannock in Staffordshire has been building and racing small hovercraft for a number of years and like several others he saw the potential of the rotary engine.

Usually most high-performance racing hovercraft use two-stroke engines such as Yamaha, Rotax, KTM, Fuji, and Hirth; but according to Bill Yates, 'The

Norton's power and good torque characteristics make it well suited to hovercraft racing. Added to this its low weight, smoothness and the potential for pressure charging also make it interesting.'

Bill has therefore, fitted two Norton aero rotary engines into his craft, a P60 for thrust and an NR731, formely known as a P73, for lift. The P60 rotary engine, which caused few problems for fitting, drives the thrust fan through a timing belt reduction gear. A 'Supertrap' absorption silencer and an extractor are routed through the side of the hull. An additional auxiliary silencer can be fitted to the rear of the craft if further noise reduction is felt to be necessary.

'The lift engine presented more of a challenge. The dust and grit thrown up by hovercraft meant that it was necessary to provide some means of filtration rotor cooling. To overcome the resistance of the filters, a small centrifugal fan was fabricated and mounted on the drive side of the eccentric shaft above the lift fan. A recoil starter was mounted in place of the oil metering pump. A new pump drive went through the centre of the starter and the pump was mounted on the starter body. It was also necessary to modify the ignition system to facilitate easy starting with the pull-start.'

In use, the P60 proved to be very reliable but there were a few problems with the P73 which had an annoying habit of stopping at race meetings. This was eventually traced to the mounting angle of the Tillitson carburettor; once this had been altered, the craft became very competitive and reliable.

'Despite our rather slow start to the season, we have still managed to finish second in the National Formula One Championship, actually winning two more meetings than the champion.' No doubt Bill will be seeking the championship title with renewed vigour next season, Good luck, Bill!

RIGHT **Norton trumpets its achievements with the air-cooled rotor in a press release. Longer term, they also pointed out that the engine is best suited to 'wide-cut' gasolene, with a high yield per barrel of crude oil.**

BELOW **Bill Yates in action.**

NORTON MOTORS LIMITED

Lynn Lane
Shenstone, Lichfield
Staffordshire WS14 0EA
Tel: 0543 480101
Telex No. 335998 NORTON
Fax No. 0543-481128

DWG/FAP/ACH-010

8 September 1989
Issue 2.

NORTON ACHIEVEMENTS WITH THE
AIR-COOLED-ROTOR TYPE OF ROTARY ENGINE

1. Approximately 2500 rotary engines manufactured.

   - All engines have low parts-count and require low investment to manufacture.

2. Twin Rotor 90 bhp motorcycle engine in production.

   - Vibration-free.
   - Very low maintenance.
   - Fuel consumption similar to the best 4 cylinder 4-stroke reciprocating type.

3. NR731 - air-cooled drone engine in production.

   - 38 bhp from 10 kg weight.
   - Low SFC (0.52 lb/bhp hour at cruise).

4. NR642 - 90 bhp light aircraft engine.

   - Now at field trial stage.
   - Integrated reduction gearbox.
   - 90 bhp for 60 kg total weight.
   - Low maintenance requirements.
   - Cruise SFC of only 0.51 lb/bhp hour.
   - Leaded or unleaded, Avgas or Mogas fuels.

5. NR801 - Ultra light and compact liquid cooled RPV engine.

   - Now in pre-production stage
   - 40 bhp at 6000 RPM or 50 bhp at 7500 RPM.
   - Weight 23 kg including integrated 1.5 kw alternator.

6. P90 - 654 cc single rotor automotive research engine.

   - Lighter, more compact and lower parts count than Mazda RX7.
   - SFC of 15% lower than Mazda RX7 engine already recorded.

7. Ultra-high performance racing engine.

   - 150 bhp at 10,500 rpm from simply - modified existing hardware.

Company No. 794608. Registered in England.
Registered Office: 5 Albemarle Street, Mayfair, London. W1X 3HF

The air-cooled rotary engine: note the deep finning around the engine housing.

Marine Applications

Exploration of the marine application has only recently been undertaken with Norton acquiring a preliminary licence for marine applications to Mercury Marine, a subsidiary of the Brunswick Corporation in the United States, which in investigating the use of rotary engines as alternatives to two stroke and four stroke engines for outboard engine configuration. Their project, due to be completed by 1992, is focussed on comparing exhaust emissions, fuel economy, power-to-weight ratio and manufacturing costs to conventional two stroke and four stroke engines.

In this country Lancing Marine based at Lancing on the south coast are working on a racing motorboat powered by a Norton rotary engine, but to date no details have been released.

Industrial and Leisure Applications

The need for light weight, compactness and the ability to digest low grade fuels for use in powering pumps and generators that are man-portable, is seen as a market of great opportunity by Norton.

For some time Norton rotary engines have been used for leisure and sport vehicles such as swamp buggies, snow mobiles and dune buggies. The compact size, exceptional smoothness and light weight has obvious potential for generator uses in mobile homes.

CHAPTER

The Classic

By 1975, the mechanical side of what was to become the Classic was finalised. The project was then turned over to designers Mike Oldfield and Bob Trigg to add suitable styling. The result of their work is shown in the photograph, with the 1976 yellow and green finished prototype. Note the pads located on the top of the side panels, 'added for a touch of luxury!'

While a whole range of styling exercises were being prepared from the mid 1970s into the 1980s, (see pp 70–74) in 1983 the company took advantage of a government-funded scheme being offered through the Department of Trade and Industry, whereby the services of design consultants were made available to suitable applicants under the Design Council's consultancy scheme. Norton were offered the services of a young design company, Dick Powell Design, for a funded fifteen-day consultation. Their brief was to assist Norton in adapting their new machine to accept a water-cooled version of the rotary engine that had been developed alongside the air-cooled engine, to help solve the perennial cooling problems.

Dick Powell Design began their consultancy work in the summer of 1983 at what was considered to be a very late stage in the design process, restricted by the fact that many components were already tooled for production. A visit was made to the factory at Shenstone on July 11 to get a review of the project and establish the best means of carrying out the task. As a result it was decided that instead of drastic action it would be better if Norton continued working with Mark White (see p 72) on the water-cooled prototype. Dick Powell Design's sole objective was to ensure that Norton had the right product in the market. They would then present a report assessing the existing design, its advantages and disadvantages, its positioning in the market place, its faults and any problems. Armed with results of this work they would then make design recommendations based upon a bare rolling chassis; recommendations utilising available parts where possible (namely the pre-tooled tank, seat, tail-unit and side panels); and where necessary make design recomendations for instruments, controls, etc.

As a starting point, Dick Powell and his partner Richard Seymour decided that they should first both road-test the air-cooled prototypes themselves. They would then look at the water-cooled styling prototype before analysing their findings for both machines, and

produce a document with their recommendations.

The first road test was conducted by Richard Seymour using an un-faired air-cooled machine. He found that on first inspection the machine was very similar in appearance to the late Commando roadster, having a narrow tank, comfortable saddle, and a good relationship between the positioning of the handlebars, seat and footpeg. In fact, in Richard's words, it felt very 'Nortonish'. On starting, the machine was found to be notchy in getting it into first gear, but once in gear the slick operating clutch allowed a smooth takeoff. The tickover apparently 'hunted' and a noticeable 'step' in power was noted when the engine revs increased. A surge of power came in the last 2–3,000 revs before and through the redline.

The braking system was praised for its good response even after heavy use, its positive feel and the fact that it did not lock up easily. Handling characteristics were considered worthy of comparison with the Norton tradition – responsive, accurate and neutral, summed up by Richard as 'pointability'.

This first road test session was then followed by a second, held on August 29, 1983, when faired and unfaired machines were made available for direct comparison. After riding the faired version that was fitted with Bill Town's petrol tank, Richard Seymour found that the machine performed very heavily in comparison to its un-faired partner. The seat-to-tank fitting was faulted for the uncomfortable riding position that it dictated. The fairing itself was also criticised for holding in heat and noise (a somewhat unfair comment as any full type fairing will reflect back both noise and heat from the engine).

Turning to the un-faired machine that had been ridden previously, this time the long period needed to warm the machine up with the choke before moving off was pointed out. Dick Powell found that he echoed the comments made by his partner but also levelled criticism at the rear suspension units; he felt they would require more facility for making adjustments than the units found on the prototype. Handlebar adjustment was also desirable. This would make the machine far more rider-friendly.

An appraisal was then made of the water-cooled prototype that was being prepared, and from a designer's view the first reactions were not very favourable. Both Dick and Richard felt that the

THIS PAGE **Prototype Classic, as styled by Mike Oldfield.**

RIGHT **Between 1976 & 1978 Norton experimented with a whole range of styling designs for a civilian rotary motorcycle. In the early 1980s, William Towns was brought in to design a sports tourer along the lines of the BMW RS.**

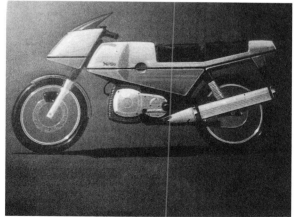

TOP LEFT Wind tunnel testing at MIRA.

TOP RIGHT Tony Denniss with a clay prototype showing experimental light cluster.

ABOVE Mark White, a student at Lancaster Polytechnic, submitted this design as part of his final year studies.

OPPOSITE ABOVE A royal appraisal of the Harris Mann design. It takes a very observant eye to see that this is not a real machine but a clay model on a chassis base.

RIGHT The tape design, one of the earliest stages of motorcycle design, requiring a high degree of skill and visual interpretation.

machine was too 'Bitty' in its appearance. The styling was a mixture of the modern, 'slabby' look and old-style engine cases, wheels, mudguard, and, in particular, the long, drain pipe-style exhaust/silencer system, a look that had gone out of fashion years earlier. Mark White's handlebar-mounted fairing, featuring twin headlamps was praised for its balancing of the machine's proportions and the way that it related to the rest of the machine.

A Question of Style

Criticism was also levelled at the old-fashioned styling of the petrol filler cap, the radiator and the complete styling of the engine unit itself. The curious mixture of styles reflected in the engine, a chain case resembling that of a BSA Rocket III and the water-pump housing of a modern 1980s two stroke, was in part because of the long period of time over which the engine had been developed. Dick Powell Design felt that more should, be made of the fact that the engine was a rotary engine, rather than obscuring this with a blend of styling from reciprocating engines.

The harshest criticisms were those levelled at the finished quality of the machine. The finishing of detailed parts unrelated to the machines function, (such as hand-painted pin-striping) had been the mark of quality in the past. But the 1980s interpretation of quality was for the machine and all its detail parts to be functional, an aesthetic that had been ignored.

In conclusion, Dick Powell Design felt that although the machine was similarly styled to the BMW RS100, they did not believe that the machine should be marketed as a 'Sports Tourer'; the engine's sporty power delivery and machine handling suggested more of a 'comfortable sports bike'. For marketing purposes they also felt that a change of graphics and livery was necessary. A set of examples emphasising and illustrating this point was given using the experience of Mercedes and Porsche cars, then Italian and German high power motorcycles. They recommended that the livery of the new Norton machine should utilise the single colour scheme used so successfully by the German and Italian manufacturers. The idea was to portray an image of quality, performance, power and luxury.

It is well known that the colour black makes things appear smaller; Dick Powell Design recommended this single colour livery, with components picked out in gloss black or in satin black. All lettering and graphics would be satin or matt black on a gloss black background. An alternative would be to use a less aggressive approach adopting an Italian motorcycle style with bodywork in one colour off-set by things such as the screen, beading, grab rail, etc, in black.

The name or model description was the next question. Most modern machines are known by an acronym, such as the GSXR750 Suzuki, FZR1000 Yamaha, GPZ600 Kawasaki, BMW K75, etc. To follow this line Dick Powell Design suggested the ATR 80, Advanced Trochoidal Rotor, which they felt reflected the forward-looking, high technology characteristics of the Norton. The suffix 80 would indicate brake horse power developed, which for a middle weight machine was very respectable. With the introduction of new models the figure could be altered accordingly.

Dick Powell Design further suggested changes to the Norton logo, although this was not part of their brief. They believed that if the machine had been released between 1971 and 1976, the logo could have remained unchanged. By 1983 it was felt that a new style logo should be used. If the logo remained the same it would be associated not only with the heyday of the British motorcycle industry, but also with its collapse. If the logo was subtly altered, it would be more up-to-date but it would not alienate the older Norton enthusiasts. A complete change, on the other hand, would reflect the revolution in the company.

There were many other minor recommendations supported by renderings and design sketches concerning components such as coils, indicators, the horn and the outdated hinged mudguard.

Criticism was made of the grab rail which had too small a gap to allow adequate grip for the pillion passenger wearing gloves, the prototype featured gaiters which also dated the styling of the machine. Criticism had also been levelled at the shock absorbers after the first road test and various alternatives were outlined. The large slab radiator had already been faulted and suggestions were made for using two smaller units to blend in with the machine.

Finally, the small quarter fairing came under scrutiny; although the design by Mark White was found to be satisfactory, its mounting was questionable. Mark's design had the fairing handlebar-mounted and Norton tested the design satisfactorily at up to 130 mph. At that time, however, the motorcycle press was damning of handlebar-mounted fairings, saying that they were unstable. Dick Powell Design favoured frame mounting as a more aerodynamic and integrated system.

Longer Term Recommendations

Mid-term recommendations were made as to future development concerning items that would be too expensive or difficult to alter at that late stage of development. The report emphasised that these further

ABOVE LEFT **Harris Mann's vision never progressed further than the clay model.**

LEFT **The 1976 machine with a William Towns tail end.**

ABOVE Endurance prototype which was tested at MIRA by Bob Rowley. A planned trip to Italy for testing was cancelled for lack of funding.

RIGHT Log book, which was signed by the MD, Director of Engineering and Quality Control Manager.

FAR RIGHT The Classic brochure: 'only 100 riders required'.

modifications were necessary either to enhance the modern appearance of the machine or to improve its ergonomics.

The footpeg bracket castings were felt to be out of character with the rest of the machine's appearance because they were too detailed; future castings should be simpler. Styling for the primary chain case and the charge transfer port needed to be more modern and renderings were submitted to assist in future design. The prototype featured a chrome-plated front mud guard which again dated the machine, as most manufacturers had turned to lighter GRP (glass reinforced plastic) units.

A close fitting GRP mudguard would add to the sporty looks of the machine, as would a cast grab rail rather than the old fashioned tubing unit then in place.

With the constant changes in motorcycle styling taking place at this time, even the wheels came in for consideration. The original design featured narrow spoked cast wheels but it was felt that these could be replaced by suitable alternatives painted so as to match the livery.

In the long term, the report recommended that if a Mark II water-cooled version was envisaged the ma-

chine would need to be designed from the ground up to produce a more singular, purposeful styling: either as a full touring machine, featuring a full fairing, with panniers incorporated into the styling; or a full sports motorcycle with a more potent version of the engine, (which Dick Powell Design felt would be the correct line to pursue).

The report concluded that overall the machine was mechanically a quality, high performance, well engineered piece of work, superior to its market rivals in a number of ways. The machine felt lighter, gave better handling and the engine was very responsive, making the motorcycle enjoyable to ride. But the problem was that these good points were let down by the outdated appearance and details, such as the five-year-old Suzuki switch gear.

The report was completed and submitted to Norton at the beginning of September 1983. After several meetings of senior management, it was shelved, with no decision taken. Yet work continued on variations in styling. The work done by the design consultants had not been wasted: it would come into its own a little later in the story . . .

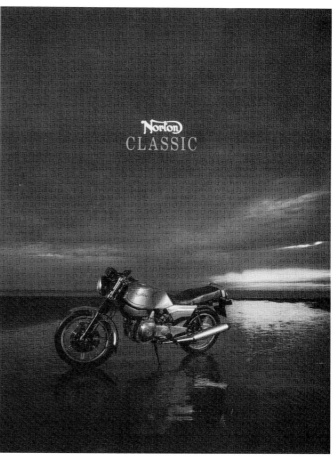

Preparing the Market

One of the stipulations that Dennis Poore had made in the early days of the rotary development work was that any machine that went into production should have a proven record of reliability. In keeping with this philosophy it was decided that an air-cooled engine endurance race prototype would be built. This machine would be used for high speed testing and long distance reliability trials to convince the press and public of the ability of the rotary engine. When a civilian machine was eventually launched it could be done so with the results of this testing to back its reliability claims.

Bob Rowley rode the machine for 24 hours at Thruxton in 1982, a demonstration organised to attract press attention to the reliability of the machine. In another demonstration at MIRA, assisted by Fred Swift as his mechanic, he covered 1,000 miles at an average speed of 135 mph, Top speed was around 140 mph which in those days was good. Bob recalls, 'All we did was put fuel and oil in the bike.'

In addition to this unusual prototype, work continued with long distance road trials of various air-cooled civilian prototypes. The press began to feel frustrated and continually speculated on a possible launch. So by the early 1980s Norton had a civilian prototype machine based upon the air-cooled Interpol II. But the company – undergoing changes at management – delayed committing themselves to a production date. In 1983, the government introduced a 10% purchase price levy, 'car tax' on the sales price of new machines, which certainly didn't help.

Launch dates were set and then postponed. At this time, no name had been given to the machine although a persistent rumour was that the machine would be called, the 'Aurora'. It was said that Dennis Poore suggested the name of the Roman goddess of dawn, the Managing Director wishing to present the new machine as the herald of the new dawn of rotary machines. But the machine that he had in mind for that role would be a totally new motorcycle in all respects: the machine that did eventually appear in December 1987 was that designed back in 1976 with a Bill Towns-styled tail light cluster. The tank and side panels were also altered. This was believed to have been the work of Doug Barber. It was felt at the time that there was a strong following in the market for a traditional machine uncluttered by panniers. The name 'Classic' was therefore chosen.

The angular lines of the Classic. Note the deep finning around the engine housing.

After the change of ownership of Norton in January 1987 things began to happen. The head of the new consortium Phillipe Le Roux discovered the prototype ready and waiting: he took a calculated gamble on the production of a limited number of these machines to establish the market reaction. After careful consideration of the financial cost of such an exercise, it was decided that 100 of the air-cooled machines would be built. Each one of the hand-built machines was individually numbered from one to a hundred.

Each owner would be presented with an individual 'log book' signed by Phillipe Le Roux, David Garside (Director of Engineering) and Bob Rowley (Quality Control Manager).

The price was £5,950 which placed it in the upper price range of machines at this time. When the sales order book of the machine was opened, (the bike was only available through the factory), Norton were flooded with cheques and sales for the limited 100 were complete within a week. The delivery date for the first machines was set for December 1987, marking an 11-year absence from the market since the demise of the Commando.

In addition to the Classic, work had accelerated on the first para-military water-cooled machines so that they were available in October of the same year.

Project P52: the Commander

As the classic went into production, Philippe Le Roux re-commissioned the young design company whose report he had read on first taking over the company.

In 1983, Dick Powell linked up with his present partner Richard Seymour, to form Seymour-Powell.

The industrial design partnership nowadays has a wide range of clients, including famous names such as Clairol, ICI, Philips, Racal, Tefal, and Yamaha. Much of the partnership's present work, for companies such as Yamaha, is involved in coming up with new concepts and prototypes for products in the future, five or even ten years along. Their aggressively productive, market-based approach to design work must have been something that attracted Philippe Le Roux; (though it sometimes upsets the traditionalists – remember that their critique of Norton marketing strategy pre-Classic had been rapidly shelved).

The MD wanted Seymour-Powell to assist Norton in producing a coherent strategy for product design, planning and marketing for the motorcycle side of the business. Initially, Norton wished to improve the Interpol II, and then launch a civilian version. In the long term, Norton recognised that they might need to branch out into a new sector of the market with a more specialised machine.

Accepting the commission and with these ideas in mind S/P first wanted an update on the developments that had taken place within the company since their last visit over four years earlier. They then wanted to road test the bikes themselves and talk to the people involved to gain an overall impression, before they began their preparation of a 'pre-design appraisal'.

The report, completed by June, covered the following points: the problems that needed to be rectified on the Interpol II, company positioning and strategy for the nineties, the concept of a new paramilitary machine, the development of a sports bike, and further suggestions for the company's long term planning.

As this report formed an integral part in the development of the water-cooled, paramilitary Commander, it is worth looking at in some detail. Apart from the Interpol II improvements and the groundwork for its civilian counterpart, reactions to a completely new sports machine could be gauged through ad hoc interviews with interested parties whilst a loaned machine was being road tested during the TT on the Isle of Man.

The mechanical problems were considered to be of such concern that they were listed at the front of the report. When these had been sorted – and only then – could any strategy, product planning, or design take place.

'The gear box is not designed or built to handle high horse power. The gearbox can be beefed up to reduce the problems with output at 85 bhp but there is obvious uncertainty as to the service life of such a unit. For future use and no doubt higher power output a new box is required.' To save valuable design and development time it was recommended that a suitable design should be bought from either BMW or a Japanese manufacturer.

The electrical system was a major source of failures due in large part to the constant modifications needed to meet police requirements. The use of two-tone horns, blue lamps and main lights added to the drain of the radio exerted a great strain. Idling problems had been apparent at an early stage and these had been more or less cured through installing a heavier fly wheel, although further investigation was advocated in looking at ignition control.

Overheating with the new water-cooled engine was not expected, although it was advised that testing be carried out at slow escort speed, high speed and for general duties in heavy traffic in hot countries, to see if an extra fan might be needed, or heat deflection from the rider when stationary.

Attention then turned to company positioning. Norton's leading role in the design, development and manufacture of rotary engines should be maintained. In support of this positioning, the company should continue to pursue its business of manufacturing rotary-engined motorcylces. This would mean restructuring the company into two corporate entities – Rotec Ltd (responsible for engine development, design, manufacturing, consultancy and licensing) and Norton Motors Ltd (responsible for the design, development, manufacture and marketing of motorcycles).

The potential for development with the rotary engine in various applications (such as aircraft engine replacement) is obviously greater than that offered by the motorcycle business. Seymour-Powell advocated more emphasis on this side of the business. The status of the motorcycle itself was changing at this time: instead of being a form of practical transport it was becoming a

Richard Seymour (LEFT) and Dick Powell in their natural environment. The design team was involved with Norton well before the F1, working on plans for the Commander and analysing the company pre-Classic.

more leisure-orientated product, a symbol of affluent freedom, which was reflected in the price. Leisure vehicles such as ATVs, (All Terrain Vehicles), micro-lights, personal hydrofoils, dune buggies, golf carts, and motor mowers were all mentioned as possible markets.

Rotec should develop so that its rotary engine skills would be the company's major product, selling its expertise to customers, in addition to maintaining its in-house ability to develop prototypes and production engines. This would mean that the company would move away from manufacturing engines in numbers and concentrate on more specialised development work. A good example of the principle is Yamaha, who have become leading experts on engine top-end design, specialising in combustion chambers and valves; their expertise is bought by many car manufacturers.

The report then moved on to Norton in the nineties. If the company was to re-establish any kind of presence in the motorcycle market it needed to build on the following factors:

1 *The Norton name* – its historical association with high standards of machine handling and performance.
2 *The rotary engine* – its power, smoothness, refine-ment and reliability.
3 *Quality of design*, engineering and finish.

For reasons of cash flow there would need to be two separate financial strategies: the first would be short-term, aimed at generating and maximising the potential of the paramilitary machine at home and abroad. The second would be longer-term, aimed at producing a completely new machine capable of ensuring Norton's future as a motorcycle manufacturer.

Consolidation in the Paramilitary Market

Norton were already in the paramilitary market (and still are). The bike itself was not considered adequate for general release as a tourer, a sports tourer, or anything else. If Norton stayed with the non-civilian market, servicing and sales could be carried out at the factory which obviated the need for a dealer network. Competition in the market was limited, with key buyers making the decisions and Norton therefore limited their exposure. In Seymour-Powell's opinion, it would be a mistake to launch a civilian machine based upon the existing bike as this would muddy the waters for future development and possibly undermine the company's fragile reputation. By concentrating on the paramilitary machine, Norton could thus build a much needed reputation for reliability without compromising long-term positioning.

Consideration was given to the formation of a completely separate project team to carry out all paramilitary work: to solve the problems on the air-cooled police machine, then reduce servicing and warranty work on these to a minimum; to expand into the paramilitary market as much as possible; and then produce a water-cooled machine specifically aimed at the paramilitary market, not for general release to the civilian market. The machine should be based as much as possible on existing designs and stock, with only the absolute minimum changes necessary to incorporate the water-cooled engine. It would also be necessary to streamline production methods and reduce costs as much as possible to increase profitability.

To achieve this, bearing in mind the market, and the limited production numbers, a new, full-protection fairing of pressed glass reinforced plastic (GRP) was recommended. This would give a good internal and an external finish and be light in weight. It should have a liner specifically designed to accommodate police instrumentation and other specific requirements.

An up-to-date tank, seat, tail and side panel design were also advised. To save costs, a cheap, cut-and-fold tank could then be covered by a one-piece all-enveloping bodywork that reached down as far as the side-panels and also included the rear lights. It would be designed to included the latest Krauser panniers and top box as well as an integral seat. Access to the machine would be gained by unclipping the rear light connectors and hinging up or removing the bodywork. Attention should also be given to incorporating panniers, top boxes with police equipment, radios, beacons, and other high visibility lights.

A dual fan set-up was a possibility, subject to the results of testing in a hot climate. Detailed attention should also be focussed on servicing requirements: easy access to aid spark plug or oil changes, etc.

At this point, Seymour-Powell strongly advised against releasing this or any other paramilitary machine for civilian use. The high costs inevitable of designing and tooling were not worth it on an outdated machine.

What they did advocate was that *if* the machine, which was essentially a tourer and not a sports tourer, was launched onto the civilian market, it should be done so in a very low key manner. The suggested sales pitch was 'Norton bow to public pressure and *reluctantly* offers for sale a *limited* number of the Interpol II machine'. With such a sales pitch the objectives would be to take advantage of the enthusiasm for such a machine, sell a limited number, which generates income, but almost as important generates interest in Norton's development programme. What they should not do was to yield to the temptation to launch the machine as the long-awaited 'civilian machine': it must only be sold as a Paramilitary machine modified by demand for civilian use.

Seymour-Powell were most concerned that any motorcycle design and development should take full advantage of the Wankel concept so as to provide support for other rotary applications and help demonstrate its main features of good power-to-weight ratio, smoothness, simplicity and reliability. To this should be added the perception of the Norton name. In the past, its reputation for good handling was largely gained through racing and early road machines. This reputation had very little to do with engineering excellence, nor, unfortunately, reliability: both these virtues had anyway became the exclusive province of the Japanese manufacturers, Norton had to wake up to the fact that their machine was very mediocre in the handling stakes when compared to the opposition.

What Norton should be aiming for was to produce a fast, lithe, lighter, sports machine, one capable of fine handling, although not necessarily capable of top speeds in excess of 150 mph (as some of the Japanese machines are). The top speed of a sports machine is purely academic considering the speed limits and penalties in most countries. Of paramount concern should be the handling of the machine.

Keep the Engine, Lose the Rest

As Norton considered commiting to a new sports machine, what was the motorcycle market like? In the late 1980s the market was still only a shadow of its former self, sales were still declining. The Japanese led the market but they were suffering from reduced sales, over-stocking, excessive model diversification, and widely fluctuating exchange rates. They had realised that the market had changed; cheap motorcycle transport which was heavy on production investment, with workable profit margins for the dealer, was out. In were higher value style (or style victim) machines with sustainable margins. This is what created the trend toward race replica's such as the Suzuki GSX–R750, high-priced super sports bikes such as the Honda RC30, muscle bikes like the Yamaha V Max, Paris-Dakars such as the Kawasaki Tangai, trikes, quads, boulevard cruisers, lightweight super sports, etc. People are prepared to pay more for these types of machine than they would for more practical types of machinery. (As in the automobile market, profit margins are of course greater on upmarket machines.) The market for basic two-wheeled transport remained depressed. In addition to the Japanese, there were (and are) a number of other manufacturers catering for tastes in other areas of the market, ranging from the out-and-out limited edition sports market, Ducati, Bimota, etc, to the nostalgia of Harley-Davidson. BMW dominated the touring class with a world wide reputation for design and excellent engineering. Most of the smaller companies were highly specialised, selling very small numbers of machines, such as Harris; others operated under favourable trading conditions like Ducati-

Cagiva, which enabled them to survive.

In this sort of market, (which hasn't changed radically in the 1990s) Norton had an advantage in that they were the only manufacturers of a rotary-powered motorcycle; but even if this could be coupled with superior handling it would still not be sufficient. These qualities would need to be bolstered by a clear association with very high quality design and engineering. This could be greatly enhanced by involvement and success in racing. When this exclusive positioning was achieved, the company could then diversify its interests into other market areas such as tourers, sports tourers, off-roaders, etc. Seymour-Powell felt that it would be much easier for Norton to expand their business from this platform rather than try to gain a reputation straight off for 'tourers that handle'.

For the new sports motorcycle, the existing rolling chassis could not be used as it did not represent the latest, state-of-the-art design, performance or handling characteristics. Only the engine should remain but this would require modifications to produce even more power. The frame needed lightening and new suspension systems needed to be developed. Attention should also be given to the choice of wheels and tyres for such a machine, quality cast-alloy wheels fitted with 17 in low profile radial tyres would not only improve handling but also contribute to the racey looks.

The dated rear shock absorbers would need to be replaced by mono shock or a rising rate suspension unit which would also help tidy the styling at the rear. This change would also require the replacement of the swinging arm which was originally connected to the gearbox directly.

The fully enclosed chain was dated and could result in oil finding its way onto the rear tyre; modern 'O' ring chains would be better. It was felt that the flip-up rear mudguard was an anachronism as few people bother to try and repair a puncture at the side of the road; tyre repairs such as 'Finilec' are far more convenient. Criticism was also levelled at the clocks, switch gear, the choke control, etc. They were all dated, but this is an area where choice is limited to what is in stock with suppliers at the time. The front suspension units, Brembo disc brakes and the discs themselves were considered to be relatively adequate but Seymour-Powell felt that there should be consultation before retaining them.

The gear box was patently inadequate for the original machine, let alone a sports machine. Of all the problems of associated with developing the sports motorcycle, this was certainly the biggest and success would depend upon the new design from Norton that was expected in about eighteen months.

In summary, Seymour-Powell were recommending that Norton should build a sports bike virtually from scratch and that production concentrate on building such a machine from factored parts designed by Norton but bought in from outside contractors, (a system employed by major car manufacturers). The exceptions would be the engine of course and possibly the gear box. At a later date, Norton could review the situation to see whether it was more economical to manufacture other parts themselves or to continue with outside contractors. As with the paramilitary machine these machines would only be sold from the factory. Customers would therefore have to place an order at a show or visit Shenstone and order their machine. To foster customer loyalty each purchaser could be presented with a log book that carries information relating to the machine, such as, quality control signatures, frame numbers, owner information, service information, machine history, etc. With this method the history of the machine could be updated by the factory when the bike changed hands, was serviced, had new parts, or a new owner.

A new sales unit would be needed at Shenstone to receive and look after customers, on similar lines to that of BMW at Park Lane in London. Care of the customer is of paramount importance today to maintain loyalty to the marque.

Seymour-Powell recommended that Norton should first build four racing motorcycles. One would be for display and sales purposes only, the others would be for testing and possibly racing. Ideally, an outside company such as Harris Performance, would be commissioned to produce these, with Seymour-Powell responsible for design alongside a small project team within Norton to ensure that all targets were met. Seymour-Powell would go on to produce finished designs for the production sports machine based upon the racing machines. They would not be equipped with finished design body work but rather dressed with parts available off the shelf. By laying the project outside Norton it would hopefully proceed more quickly and also allow work on the paramilitary machine to proceed uninterrupted. Information about these machines would be leaked to the press in a very controlled way and, subject to the machines fulfilling expectations, Norton would go racing. Extreme testing at MIRA and at closed circuits would be necessary.

The racing machines should not be allowed to compete in open competition until the company was confident that they could finish in the top three without a blow-up in the early laps. How a racing programme should be put together had not been discussed: this would obviously depend upon the class in which they would be allowed to compete and what sort of profile they gave the programme. It was hoped that by then the whole PR effort would have been carefully orchestrated to show Norton Racing as 'improving the breed' with the fully finished road machine poised to move into the market place. Security on the programme would need to be maintained throughout the project to ensure its subsequent success and to this end it was felt that the existing attitude to security at Shenstone needed to be

Seymour/Powell rendering for the Commander, incorporating integral panniers.

changed. To implement the programme successfully it should be split into four distinct areas: engine development and sourcing, motorcycle design, testing and racing, and public relations.

The first of these, Engine development and sourcing, was considered to be the most crucial: without the right power output, the project would be dead before it even started. It was suggested that Brian Crighton should be made responsible for this particular area to capitalise on his existing skills. When the list of responsibilities had been finalised and agreed a budget would need to be drawn up, as well as realistic self-set targets.

Brian's first task was to test the exhaust ejector system and verify power outputs. The exhaust system had been criticised for being too big and clumsy. If necessary, outside experts could be brought in to achieve the goals of reducing both the length and noise level without reducing performance.

A major task would be to ensure that a gearbox was sourced for immediate use in the machines and to make certain that any new gearbox design was compatible with all Norton's requirements. Any excess weight would need to be trimmed from the machine wherever possible. The previously mentioned idling problems would also need to be sorted in line with optimising carburation; possibly by the use of new, lighter carburettors. In the long term, fuel injectors had to be considered. Oil separation problems would need to be

addressed to ensure that the lubrication system was fully operative. This would require more work on understanding engine cooling and David Garside's (hot spot) criticisms.

Seymour-Powell recommended that motorcycle design, be put out to a specialist company whose brief would be to design and build the race machines in close co-operation with Brian Crighton. Seymour-Powell would produce concept sketches for the road bike as soon as work on the paramilitary machine was completed, but this would not prevent design and prototype work from going ahead.

Testing and racing would require detailed programming so that all aspects of testing, from high speed work at MIRA to specific circuit testing, could be carried out most efficiently. The services of a professional rider supported by a full-time mechanic, who could also act as driver would be needed. All testing would be overseen by the project engineer Brian Crighton to ensure all objectives were reached. At this point in the report, mention was made of Brian's project, a race machine he had built based upon a blueprinted Interpol II. S/P advised that it should not be publicly raced, but that it should be added to the

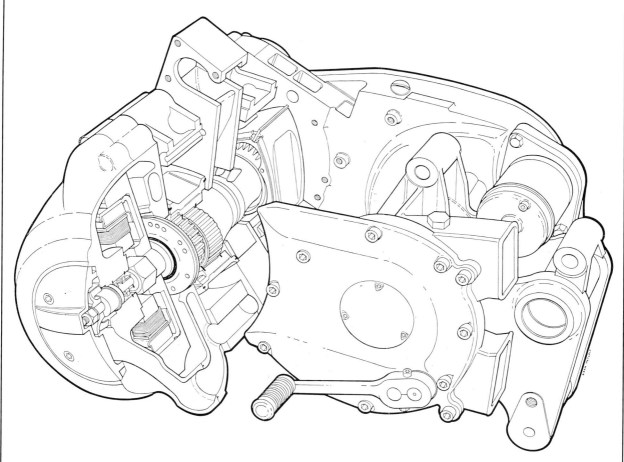

programme as a mobile test bed. A detailed race programme could be put together when it was clearly established that the machine was fully competitive.

The 'leakage' of closely guarded secrets by the PR men would be essential to the build-up of expectation. Once testing has established that reliable power was available and that the machine was fully competitive, then more, information could be released, but nothing about the final road machine should be made public so that when finally announced it would make the biggest impact.

Finally at the end of this comprehensive appraisal recommendations were given as to the long term planning of the company. The development and design of the paramilitary machines should continue as it was felt that the market would not change very much and was unlikely to disappear. Assuming that the re-vamped Interpol II machine was a reasonable success, then design work could begin on a new machine that might do double duty as a sports-tourer for the public. Sales of the sport machine should continue alongside a possible development of a less exclusive and cheaper version of the machine. Work could then progress on a sports-tourer concept that would also double as a new paramilitary machine, the emphasis being on the 'tourer that handles' as had already been mentioned earlier in the report.

Implementing the Report

The report was completed by early June and promptly submitted to Norton who decided to act upon some of the recommendations that had been made. A new paramilitary machine specifically designed for European police forces, (believed to be the first) moved from design concept to prototype within eight months and was launched in October 1987. The new machine was the Commander. It featured a water-cooled engine housed in a chassis based upon the old Interpol II chassis and used many parts supplied by Yamaha. The machine featured a number of novel design features such as a single moulded shell tank seat unit, and integral crash bar, blue strobe lights mounted behind the fairing screen, integral panniers and a 'police stop' sign set into the rear bodywork.

The rear panniers had a single lid which when opened could be left up to reveal the radio and clipboard storage space on the top of the rear mudguard. The rear lights themselves were Opel Corsa light units turned upside down. These helped determine the

ABOVE LEFT The water-cooled
Norton Wankel engine;
cooling has always been more
than half the battle with
rotary engines.

ABOVE The Commander was
tested by police forces across
the country; the riders praised
it, but the purchase price was
higher than for the BMW,
which depressed orders.

RIGHT The water-cooled
housing with eccentric shaft.

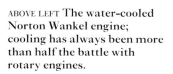

FAR LEFT Necessarily powerful rear lights for police work.

LEFT Top view of integral panniers, with carrying capacity of 25 litres each.

BELOW LEFT The cockpit with Yamaha instrumentation, as easy to read at night (RIGHT). Paramilitary version left, civilian right.

BELOW Two batteries are necessary for the machine's paramilitary role, for powering radio, two-tone horn, lights etc.

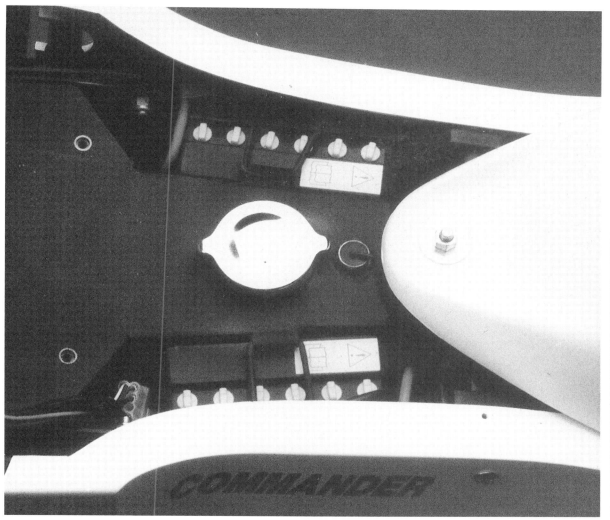

LEFT The distinctive and imposing Commander profile: but the machine does not ride as heavily as it looks.

ABOVE Commander in use by the West Midlands Police, who were involved with the machine from the outset.

RAC's 'knights of the road' motorcycles are used to reach breakdowns in congested urban areas.

shape of the rear panniers. It will be remembered that the S/P report had emphasised that production costs should be kept down by using off-the-shelf parts wherever possible; this was obviously put into practice. Following this advice, the 37 mm, steel braced front forks and front and rear wheels came from the Yamaha XJ900; switches, clocks, front, rear disc brakes and callipers also came from the same source. When Yamaha launched the XJ900 as a sports/tourer, for some reason it never really took off, despite being an adequate performer with a budget price. As a result they had large quantities of parts that were redundant until they were acquired by Norton for use on the Commander. To power the radio, two batteries were fitted to the machine on either side of the oil tank, which was an integral part of the monocoque frame.

When the order book for the Commander was opened to the 51 police forces throughout the country in October 1987, a number of the machines were offered for testing with the option to buy. A significant number of the police forces had already expressed their interest in the new machine and eventually thirty five police forces took up the option of testing the machine. For the police motorcyclist, the Commander was what many had been waiting for. The machine was extremely comfortable to ride during the long periods out on traffic patrol and the lack of vibration from the engine helped to reduce rider fatigue.

Despite the popularity of the machine with the riders, some forces have continued with their fleets of BMW machines mainly for financial reasons. The initial cost of the Commander is slightly higher than that of BMW who are able to give a discounted price because of the larger volume of machines that they produce. Other reasons were given. It would require expensive re-tooling of police garages to cope with the servicing of the machines, and re-training of mechanics and fitters. There would be engine problems if a police rider failed to keep the oil tank filled. The replacement of the bodywork would be expensive as there are no integral crash bars fitted or means of attaching these to the front of the Commander: in some situations the rider may be required to lay the machine down and the BMWs fitted with crash bars are able to withstand this with only minor damage to the crash bars and mirrors.

A number of the machines have also been bought by the Department of Defence for various roles with the armed services. Other buyers include the West Midlands ambulance service and the Royal Automobile Club who use the machines as rapid response units.

The civilian version of the machine was revealed on May 25 1988 at a London launch, followed by a major launch in the Isle of Man at the Villa Marina during the TT races. This was planned to cash in on the expected race successes of the RCW588 on the island that summer.

Riding the Commander

First impression on seeing the Commander is that it is a big, heavy machine but this idea is soon dismissed when you take the machine off its main stand. The weight of the machine (513 lbs) is low down when you sit into the machine, rather than on it, everything feels nicely balanced. Actual riding position is dictated by the seat contours, handle bar and foot peg configuration which promotes a sit-up stance like that of a police motorcyclist. I had expected this style of riding position to be uncomfortable, especially over a long distance, but after 140 miles of fast riding it was nice to still feel totally comfortable. No wonder the Commander is so popular with police motorcyclists.

Looking forward, the screen is just below eye level but the view through it is optically very good, instrumentation is from the Yamaha stock room and provides clear rider information, including direction indicator warning lights, oil warning light, main beam warning light, neutral indicator, speedometer, tachometer, engine temperature gauge, fog lights, an accurate fuel gauge and a useful digital clock. There is also a recess in the front of the fairing for the location of a radio unit if this is required.

The handlebars and the foot pegs are both adjustable to suit individual rider's preferences and all the switches and controls are easily operated even with heavy motorcycle gloves on. For starting the machine

Completed machine awaiting fitment of tank, seat unit, etc.

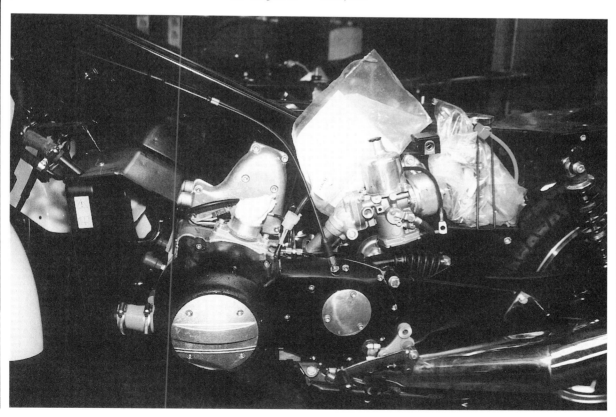

ABOVE **Rider's view; not very different to the paramilitary version.**

ABOVE LEFT **Swinging arm assembly of the Commander.**

BELOW LEFT **The civilian Commander, showing its clean, sweeping lines. The screen affords excellent protection in poor weather.**

from cold, the choke is operated by a four position, rotary switch on the left handlebar. Turning the ignition switch on, rotating the choke towards you to the first or second position and pressing the starter, the machine whirrs into life first time. As it fires into life, with a puff of blue smoke and its characteristic two-stroke-like exhaust note, the smoke reveals the fact that the engine has a total loss lubrication system. The machine features a safety cut-out on the side stand so that if you try and start the machine with the side stand down an ignition cut-out prevents the engine from running. The engine does require several minutes operation on the choke before it is happy for the choke to be released and first gear smoothly engaged.

Opening up the throttle very gently and releasing the clutch, the machine picks up quickly due to the excellent low down torque and moves off with the uncanny lack of mechanical vibration. Once on the move, as you go up through the gears, the engine pulls strongly through the rev range with the 'electric motor' smoothness which is the hall mark of the rotary engine. As the engine is so smooth, it has been necessary to fit a rev-limiter that operates at 9500 rpm, some 500 rpm above the level at which maximum power is developed. Maximum engine torque is found at around 7,000 rpm and keeping below this level will ensure maximum engine life. It does take time to remember that once in top the engine can be slowed without coming down through the gears, so instead of changing down for roundabouts you only need to drop the revs, apply the brakes to lose forward speed and then having negotiated the roundabout you just roll the revs back on, so the torque accelerates you smartly away. Being able to use the highest gear for the type of riding required will help improve fuel consumption, reduce wear in the engine, gearbox, final drive, tyres, etc, and helps reduce noise.

Because of the easy, smooth application of power delivery by the rotary engine journeys take less time and are far more relaxing. The excellent fairing enables high speeds to be maintained for long periods as no turbulence reaches the rider. In heavy rain the rider is encapsulated by the wind passing around and over the rider so that little rain actually reaches the rider or pillion passenger. The more you ride this machine the more you enjoy its free revving engine so that your speed increases without you noticing: it is then that restraint has to be exercised. The machine is a touring bike and not a sports bike – it is too easy to push the

machine to the limits of its touring capacity and start criticising its lack of performance as a sports bike.

Having said this, the machine was well able to deal with fast sweeping country roads where high speed was maintained through a combination of flexibility of the engine and careful use of the brakes. The steering is fast acting and with the wide bars enables changes of line to be made without any sense of drama if the corner tightens. In comparison to similar sized motorcycles today, the tyres are relatively narrow and take a while to get used to, but the Pirelli Phantom tyres proved more than adequate both in the dry or in the wet.

As there is so little engine braking power, the braking system itself of XJ900 origin proves well able to cope with the weight and speed of the Commander. Top speed is estimated to be in the region of 125 mph with engine torque freely available well up to the 9,500 rpm red line in all the lower gears, which makes for effortless cruising at 80 to 100 + mph even with two up. In daylight hours the day time running lights proved remarkably useful in attracting driver's attention as did the impressive sounding horn. The headlight is more than adequate for fast night riding and because of the lack of vibration the rear view mirrors remain crystal clear throughout the rev range.

Placing the machine on to its main-stand is extremely easy, lifting up using the leg/pannier guard the machine rolls onto the stand with no effort. Petrol consumption is very reasonable; even when maintaining high speeds on motorways, fuel consumption remained above 40 mpg. At lower speeds this could be raised to around 50 mpg. The petrol gauge is nice and accurate so that you are kept fully aware of the petrol level, the tank holds 23 litres including a reserve of three litres. To get

ABOVE The smooth and reliable engine unit, side panel removed, showing air filter housing etc.

ABOVE RIGHT The XJ900 Yamaha front wheel of the Commander.

at it when the fuel gauge shows empty, the petrol tap's turned to 'reserve'. The petrol tap is located under the right side body panel which is removed by turning the five DZUS push turn fasteners; but most riders will soon get into the habit of re-fuelling before they reach the red line. If you do use the reserve, you should remember to re-set the petrol tap once you have re-fuelled.

Oil consumption of the single grade 40 diesel type oil averages out at 450 miles to the pint and a warning light operates when the oil tank level falls to the last litre. Following the two stroke habit of checking the oil each time you fill up with petrol will prevent the level ever reaching this mark.

For pillion passengers, the Commander offers a superb long distance mode of transport; the lack of vibration and the deeply padded seat makes for comfortable riding. The foot pegs have little vibration to transmit and so high speed cruising two-up can be maintained over long distances. Wind buffeting of the pillion passenger is virtually eliminated by the excellent screen which has a lip that diverts the air flow up and over both rider and pillion, when speeds exceed 80 plus, some wind pressure can be felt but not sufficient to be tiresome.

The luggage carrying capacity of the Commander is somewhat restricted: the two integral panniers have a load capacity of 25 litres each and there is also sufficient space at the back of the tail unit to stow a set of waterproofs. Due to the fibreglass bodywork, magnetic tank bags are redundant and there is little provision for anchoring bungees.

The price of the Commander, at the time of writing (£7,599) makes it comparable with the BMW range of machines, but it is worth considering the fact that the Commander will work out to be less expensive to run. The Norton will require fewer services than a conventional motorcycle. Reference to the owner's manual shows that apart from routine checks, basic maintenance of oil, air filter, spark plugs and other components will only be necessary every 12,000 miles or annually. Also on the plus side is the fact that the machine is simple to maintain and the time required to carry out all the routine maintenance tasks is far shorter than that associated with conventional machines, where servicing charges are high. The engine of the Commander will also last a lot longer than an ordinary engine, having fewer moving parts to wear or needing adjustment. Maintenance tasks are fully described and well illustrated in the owners manual. The machine also comes equipped with a set of tools which are amongst the best quality on-board motorcycle tools around.

Any rider must be prepared for one particular problem associated with owning a Commander: wherever you park the machine, you can virtually guarantee that within a very short period of time you will have attracted an audience. Woe betide you if you stay near the machine, for if you do, the questions will flow thick and fast, 'Is this the rotary engine Norton?' etc etc. You have been warned!

Integral pannier: attractive enough, but not a great deal of room.

ABOVE **Pre-production Classic, 1984 Isle of Man, looking very different to the final version.**

BELOW Nick Medlin did not like Norton's metallic grey, so he went to the factory with some BMW red paint for his Commander.

TOP Still looking for that big sponsor: an early Norton race machine.

ABOVE Simon Buckmaster, 1988; at Snetterton in May of that year he gained two second places, a third and a fifth.

RIGHT Trevor Nation on the Isle of Man with Carl Fogarty (centre), the man who nearly joined the Norton team in 1990.

ABOVE **Ron Haslam, getting the feel of the RCW588 at Brands Hatch, 1990.**

RIGHT **Trevor Nation 1991 – but on the 'old' machine. Taken during practice at Mallory Park.**

BELOW **Carl Fogarty leads at Snetterton, chased by Steve Spray** *et al.*

ABOVE 'Rocket' Ron Haslam tests the 1991 Norton race
machine. Compare the fairing with the shot of the
earlier machine (previous pages, above left).

RIGHT The 1991–92 Norton racing team. Barry
Symmons with his new baby, the NRS588 that Ron
Haslam is about to take around Snetterton.

ABOVE The author contemplates the British Great Black Hope of the Superbike market. The F1, under test, Spring 1991.

BELOW The International Motorcycle Show, Birmingham 1990; the F1R is on the left.

Norton's Return to Racing

Back in April 1987, a Norton rotary-powered racer existed only in the mind and imagination of aero engine development engineer Brian Crighton. Yet by April 1988, a rotary-powered machine based upon the air-cooled engine, (the same as that used in the Police 'Interpol II' and the civilian version the 'Classic') had won a number of club races in the hands of Norton test and development rider Malcom Heath and had taken Simon Buckmaster to a heat win in an ACU star championship event. Not an overnight success, but in the highly competitive world of motorcycle racing a fantastic effort. And how sweet it was to see a British motorcycle beating the Japanese.

When Brian first approached the Norton management with a proposal for developing a rotary race machine he was told to forget the idea, that there was no way that such a small company could compete with the might of the Japanese. Yet convinced of the potential of the rotary engine, Brian Crighton continued to put his proposals for a racing machine forward to the senior management at every opportunity.

As a development engineer, Brian had access to the test bed facilities which allowed him to set up a motorcycle and work on increasing the power output. Brian had built up a wealth of experience on the rotary engine through his development work for aero engines and other applications. His real skill lay in the tuning of the engine. A former racer himself, Brian had never been able to afford a proper race bike and so he had to work on his own bikes to make them competitive; this taught him many things about tuning. All extra work (with such things as port openings,) was carried out in his spare time, and at one point the project seemed to be getting out of hand. A lot of people did not think it was possible for Brian to get more than 100 bhp from the original engine, which produced 79 bhp at 9,000 rpm. An engine had been set up previously on the test bed where it had been able to produce 96 bhp, obviously insufficient power output for a racing machine. In fact, the project was shelved for a while as the pressures of Brian's official role as development engineer on aero engines increased, leaving him with no free time.

When he returned to his project he was determined to prove his theory correct. For the air-cooled, twin rotor engine, he developed a clever system of separating the induction and cooling systems. Cooling was achieved by using an exhaust venturi to create a

Destined to enter the fray for Norton Racing, Ron Haslam, riding for the team for the first time in 1991.

pressure drop that dragged cool air through the existing transfer ports. This was termed the 'Exhaust Ejector' system. The major requirement for any engine to operate at peak potential is to allow it to 'breathe' correctly. This new system avoided the intake 'labyrinth' system of the road machines that restricted engine breathing.

Brian Crighton

Brian has been called 'the father of the Norton rotary racer' a title that the man himself finds embarrasing, yet one that is true: it was his persistence in developing a race machine from a police Interpol II motorcycle that has led to the John Player Special Norton race machines challenging the might of the Japanese. 'It was always my dream to build an all-British machine that was capable of winning a World Championship.'

Brian Crighton followed a career in electronic engineering for about ten years. During his spare time he began to race motocycles and by the mid 1970s was racing a 50 cc, a 125 cc and a 500 cc machine. Work on tuning machines for racing often found him late at night fixing a garden hose into an engine and spending the next couple of hours getting soaking wet whilst he learned about porting and mixture flow. The valuable skills Brian developed in engine tuning helped him win the 50 cc World Championship three years running.

In 1983 Brian joined Norton with the service department where he began learning about the rotary engines from servicing the police Interpol IIs. After only a short time he realised that the engine had tremendous potential for racing. In only twelve months Brian became a highly respected member of the department and was promoted to the Research and Development department with David Garside, working on aero engines.

Brian started to make approaches to the management to get their backing in building a race machine. At this time no-one was interested and Brian lost heart and decided to leave to work on main frame computers. Despite having left, he was regularly consulted by the factory about engine problems and he often carried out work for them. Through this contact Brian heard that the factory was being taken over by a new management. He re-applied for a job at the factory with one proviso, that he be allowed to work on developing a race machine.

The story of the race machines really begins with Brian's return to the factory and his development of the engine's power output (which even involved designing a new ignition system). From the early trials he was closely involved and continued development work, in addition to being race team manager. The amazing success of the team led to the sponsorship from Imperial Tobacco and the appointment of a professional race team manager, which allowed Brian to concentrate on development.

But the hoped-for unity under a team manager did not materialise with Nick Colliss, and in December 1989 Barry Symmons was appointed to the post. He brought in a number of people with whom he had worked before. Up until this time, Brian had taken most of the major decisions as to how the machines should be set up; all of a sudden, he was relegated to a specific role as development technician, which could not have been easy. To his credit, he accepted the situation for the good of the team and for a time things in the Norton camp were rosy. As the season progressed however, there was a growing tension between Brian, Barry Symmons and Ron Williams. Brian had his ideas on both engine development and the special characteristics required from the chassis to handle the unique power delivery from the rotary. Ron Williams had developed a worldwide reputation for successful chassis and suspension work with a number of the major race teams and was firmly committed to the mono-shock system of rear suspension, but this conflicted with Brian's own view. Having developed the rotary engine Brian understood the way it transmitted its power, which is different to that of a two or a four stroke. He believed that the Norton rotary was more suited to a twin-shock system of rear suspension, even though this gave a somewhat dated look to the machine. Steve Spray actually rode a twin-shock machine fitted with an F1 engine running in the opposite direction at Mallory Park where he was turning in faster times than he had on the mono-shock machine the previous year.

This and other differences of opinion became increasingly intractable and so in October Brian decided that he had had enough and left the team.

Only time will tell whether Norton Racing can survive without him. Few people, if any, know as much as he does about the rotary race engine. Brian was working on a number of projects such as development work for a possible '500' version for Grand Prix racing, a fan system to replace the exhaust ejector system, a fuel injection system and a whole range of radical ideas that were never made known to Norton.

He has established with Chris Oldfield the Roton Company, which plans to produce rotary engines in Australia. This new company offers race fans the delicious prospect of JPS Nortons and Roton bikes battling it out at Grand Prix level: and Steve Spray is with them! He had his first outing for the Roton team in March 1991 at Cadwell Park, gaining a 6th and a 7th place. The Roton team intend to compete in three Grand Prix 500 cc rounds as permitted by the FIM: the Australian, the British and the Malaysian; and has already won in F1 in Australia at Oron Park (see p. 151).

ABOVE **Brian Crighton** at work with Norton, the man most responsible for the Norton rotary racer; though seen here during aero-engine reliability tests.

BELOW AND RIGHT **Brian** with Steve Spray and the new Roton.

The relatively simple 'Ram Air' system force-fed the forward facing carburettors directly from the outside through vents in the fairing, allowing the engine to breathe cleanly and significantly reduced the temperature of the intake charge. These two systems liberated enormous horsepower. To further improve the engines breathing the standard carburettors, $1\frac{1}{2}$-in constant vacuum SUs, were replaced by a pair of 34 mm smooth bore Amals.

Armed with the dynamometer results achieved so far, which showed power production to be now around 120 bhp, Brian approached the Norton chairman Philippe Le Roux for official factory support, who promptly sanctioned a prototype racer.

To help the project get underway Philippe Le Roux made a written-off police Interpol available and this became the basis for the Norton prototype rotary racer. The majority of the building work was then carried out by Brian Crighton and Dave Evans in their spare time, with support and help from other development enginers. The original frame was considered to be unsuitable for racing so this was modified by cutting the back end off and re-tubing it while attention was also given to altering the position and type of rear suspension. When the machine was finally completed after an all-night session, both Dave Evans and Bob Rowley made a grab to ride it up the factory yard. Dave won and was the first to ride; needless to say Bob had a go.

By June 1987, Brian and Dave felt that their prototype racer was ready for testing at the Motor Industries Research Association (MIRA) track near Nuneaton. The machine would be ridden by Bob Rowley who was an experienced Norton test rider. Bob took it around the test circuit, building up his speed and confidence in the machine, before putting in several quick laps, during which he recorded speeds of over 170 mph. This achievement was impressive enough to convince Philippe Le Roux to approve further funding for the project. The antics of this machine earned it the

ABOVE 'Waltzing Walter'.

LEFT Air intake housing of the 'ram air' system.
(Picture *Motor Cycle News*, 1987).

ABOVE **Malcolm Heath at Darley Moor, 1987.**

RIGHT **Early Days: Brian Crighton with Bob Rowley (Picture *Motor Cycle News*).**

nickname, 'Waltzing Walter' as it was prone to move about the track at high speed. Today it resides at the Norton race team headquarters at Shenstone.

First outing

During these initial trials, it was patently obvious that the tremendous power increase from the engine was too great for the 'standard' modified frame to cope. With a limited amount of capital, it was decided to invest in a purpose-built race frame and a set of stiffer front forks. Six weeks later a 'Mark Two' prototype, with a stiffer but lighter Spondon alloy frame and RG500 Suzuki racing Kayaba front forks, was taken to the Darley Moor race circuit. One of the reasons for choosing this circuit was the Malcolm Heath was Champion of Darley Moor; another was that it was relatively quiet. This was a circuit that was well known to Brian Crighton who had won a number of races there when he had been racing during the early seventies. In fact Brian used to race 50 cc, 125 cc and 500 cc and for three years was actually British 50 cc champion, it was during this time that he learnt most of his two and four stroke tuning skills, skills that were then applied to developing the rotary engine.

So the modified machine, in reality the first Norton rotary race machine, appeared on the starting grid at Darley Moor in the capable hands of Malcolm Heath, a club racer known to, and living close to Brian. In the race programme for the Bank Holiday Monday meeting the machine was referred to simply as a 'Norton', race number '33'. The race began with the Norton on the back row of the grid but by the end of the race it had stormed through to finish in third place. Watching the machine in its first outing were Philippe Le Roux and a number of people from the Norton factory. After the meeting, Malcolm was offered a job as the official test rider and engineer, which he duly accepted. The main reason that the machine started from the back row of the grid was that the organisers of the meeting were unsure as to which category the engine actually fitted.

Eleven days later Malcolm won two races at the fast 1.968 miles, flat circuit at Snetterton, near Thetford in Norfolk. During these first few races the appearance of the Norton rotary race machine created a lot of interest with both the race fans and the motorcycle press. Here was the long-awaited challenge to Japanese racing supremacy, a British-built machine with an unusual engine carrying the old established Norton name. Although it must be remembered that this was a very small scale, low finance, experimental exercise.

For other riders in the same race as the Norton the machine was an unknown quantity: what were its power characteristics, did it have a power band, and what capacity was the engine? With the first of its wins the inevitable rumours began to fly around the paddock;

ABOVE **Sponsorship for 1988: the red, white and blue machine was balanced by AMAL, Silkolene and Renold, amongst others.**

RIGHT **The bare bones. Neither the suspension nor the gearbox could cope with the engine's power.**

within a very short period of time Norton were supposed to have a serious problem with carburation. This rumour was partially true: the rotary racing engine is very sensitive to carburation. Stories were partly the result of the dramatic burst of flames emitted from the exhaust system when the throttle was shut quickly, highly alarming for a following rider if you were not used to it. In reality this was just a characteristic of the rotary engine's operational cycle. If one recalls the cycle of the engine, the fresh mixture enters through the peripheral port at a 10 o'clock position, the mixture then begins to be compressed in the 12 o'clock position reaching maximum compression at 3 o'clock; combustion takes place between 3 o'clock and 7.30 continuing slightly during the exhaust phase, between that a degree of overlap occurs, similar to valve overlap in a four-stroke reciprocating engine. This is due to the inlet and exhaust ports being so close together. Therefore on overrun the incoming charge can be drawn out through the exhaust port where it is ignited, producing the characteristic burst of flames.

Another rumour was that the engine did not always respond to the throttle, that it sometimes did not shut off when the throttle was closed. The problem lay with the fact that the Amal slide type carburettors did not close fast enough when the throttle was shut. The continual vacuum created inside the engine meant that even though the throttle was shut, the engine was still able to drag in more mixture than required, causing the revs to flutter; again, a characteristic of the rotary engine.

All the work carried out on the machine in these early days was based upon calculated guesswork as there was no comparative data around. Any changes that were made were done step by step. Once one thing was changed the effect that this had on the performance and handling was carefully monitored; if it did not work, it was easy to take a step back and try again. This was a policy that Brian had established in his own racing career and that he carried through to the rotary racing project, the same thinking as that of Dave Evans and

Malcolm Heath. Norton had produced a racing motor-cycle, but it still needed a lot of work doing to it. The engine was extremely powerful so its speeds were high going into corners; under heavy braking the front forks, which obviously worked very well for the Suzuki RG500, flexed badly, upsetting stability.

By now there was a growing interest in the rotary race machine and a number of top road racers actually tried the machine for themselves, such as Mick Grant who tried it out at Mallory Park. After his session he was impressed by the smooth power performance of the engine but criticised the suspension system. At the end-of-season meeting at Brands Hatch, Tim Bourne, an experienced national class racer, took the machine out and managed to set some very fast lap times. Encouraged by these early successes Norton decided to enter two machines, possibly four — if development work on the water-cooled version was completed in

time – in the TT. It was also announced that the coming season would see the launch of the Norton race team with the signing up of two well-established British, international class riders, Trevor Nation and Simon Buckmaster. They were to contest the British Formula One class championship and as a major priority the 1988 Isle of Man Senior TT, the race which Norton had dominated so much in the glory days too many years before.

During the winter months, time was spent in improving the machine ready for the next season. A new gearbox was produced to replace the earlier unit that used an old Triumph T160 Trident gear cluster originally designed by Rod Quaife. This had proved unreliable because it could not cope with the power. Continued fine tuning work by Brian Crighton on the engine now produced 130 to 140 bhp at 9,500 rpm. This was an incredible power gain of 50% to 60% over the standard road bike engine from which it had been developed.

Another improvement was a new ignition system developed by Brian. This was a Hall effect electronic ignition unit consisting of a transistor trigger unit which fires a conventional CDI unit when it detects the presence of a small bar magnet attached to the eccentric shaft. The CDI unit, being non-inductive, could supply a reliable voltage to the spark plugs at whatever rev range. This replaced the unreliable self-generating ignition system that was used to begin with.

ABOVE **Mick Grant on RCW588 (Picture *Motor Cycle News*).**

RIGHT *Motor Cycle News* **reporter Mat Oxley is pursued round Donington by (PC) Nation on a Police Commander (Picture *Motor Cycle News*, December 1988).**

Sponsorship for 1988

1988 began with early testing sessions on Dunlop tyres at Mallory Park, Brands Hatch and Snetterton, with three machines, one of which featured a new Norton-designed gearbox. Simon Buckmaster and Malcolm Heath rode the original machines whilst Trevor Nation got the new gearbox. Some sponsorship had been gained during the winter months from such people as Dymag, who manufactured the front and rear wheels, Duckham oils, Renold, the rear chain manufacturers, Amal the carburettor manufacturers and Dunlop tyres. The race effort still was only a very small concern, although the factory did fund it.

1988 began well with Simon Buckmaster winning an Auto-Cycle Union Star heat at Brands Hatch. In the final he was leading until forced to retire with battery trouble, the result of damage sustained in an earlier race. That particular race had given more encouragement to the Norton crew. Simon had crashed but to his credit he had remounted to cut back through the field to eighth place in the Euro-lantic race which featured 24

of the world's best Superbike class riders in the annual Europe versus the USA start-of-season competition. This meant that the Norton rotary was proving itself truly competitive at international level. Simon Buckmaster continued his fine performances: at Snetterton in May he scored an amazing two second places, a third place and a fifth place against Britain's top F1 riders.

The team went to the Isle of Man, where both Simon Buckmaster and Trevor Nation finished the senior TT at average speeds of over 106 mph. Trevor completed a lap of the demanding $37\frac{3}{4}$-mile circuit at a speed of over 115 mph. Yet at the TT the race machines revealed how big a problem still existed with handling, mainly owing to the suspension. On the tight, twisting confines of the often stone walled road circuit the machine became a handful to ride, even for big Trevor, who was heard to say that the machine wasn't handling correctly to the point that he was scared to put the power on properly. Attempts to cure the unpredictable handling were made by changes to the front suspension, steering rake, the fork yokes, shock absorber springs, their linkages and even the swinging arm.

Of the Isle of Man performance, Brian Crighton then the racing team manager said, 'The Isle of Man race was really more of a development effort than an attempt for outright success. The fortnight long TT race and practice period gave us more time at speed on the engines than we have ever had before and the premium placed by the Manx "Mountain" circuit on handling, braking and general reliability taught us more about the machine than a whole season of normal racing'.

Suspension solution

Under racing conditions the suspension system of any race machine is subjected to tremendous forces with which it has to cope to keep the wheels in contact with the track surface. But unlike other race machines, the rotary power of the Norton behaved differently. As Brian Crighton explains, 'The bike is unique in terms of its suspension requirements. The engine has an almost flat torque curve, therefore accelerating hard out of corners was having the effect of jacking down the rear suspension. This produced huge wheelies exiting

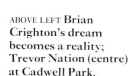

ABOVE LEFT Brian Crighton's dream becomes a reality; Trevor Nation (centre) at Cadwell Park.

LEFT Team rider Simon Buckmaster checks his rear tyre at the same meeting.

ABOVE Pre-race tension, with Malcolm Heath.

RIGHT Success!

bends, light steering in corners and reduced track bump absorption whilst under power.'

The Italian F1 front forks they were now using were clearly not able to cope with the characteristics of the rotary engine's performance and needed replacement, as did the rear Ohlins. According to race mechanic Dave Hickman. 'The machine would flatten the suspension yet still the rear of the machine would squat under power, however stiff the springs fitted were.' Work was therefore concentrated on solving the suspension problems; the engine was raised two inches in the frame and the wheelbase was slightly shortened.

The solution to the problem eventually came from Stuart Hickin, the White Power suspension expert, who was brought into build a special unit that could deal with the unusual characteristics of the rotary. With plenty of information from Brian, Dave and Trevor as to what was needed, Stuart developed a unit that drastically revised compression damping and dramatically transformed the handling, especially when this was matched with a set of upside-down front forks. By August 6 these significant changes had been made to both the front and rear suspension for the British Championship F1 race at the British Grand Prix held at Donington Park. A set of White Power 'upside-down' front forks and a rear mono-shock unit helped Trevor Nation to third place, despite a poor start. In doing so he set a new F1 lap record of 1 minute 40.5 seconds to the delight of the 60,000 watching fans. The Norton rider had in fact sliced an amazing 1.2 seconds off the old lap record that had been set by Roger Marshall during the 1987 World Championship F1 race.

In addition to the changes in suspension there were also modifications in the engine. The distance of the support race in which the Norton was entered was thirty laps, longer than the normal races, so a fuel pump was fitted to ensure the fuel lasted the race distance. The pump performed its task well and it also provided a bonus in that it delivered a constant flow of fuel and oil that made carburation with the Amal smoothbores far more consistent.

A week later, racer Andy McGladdery was invited to race the same machine at Carnaby, as Trevor Nation was in hospital for a skin graft on a leg he injured in a moto-cross crash, and Simon was racing in the Swedish Grand Prix at Anderstorp. Andy won the 1300 Star race and gave the Norton team its first open class National victory but only after race leader Steve Spray was Black-flagged when his rear caliper broke. In a second 1300 race Andy further delighted the Norton fans by winning again.

This was followed by further successes for Trevor Nation at his home circuit Thruxton where he claimed his first National win and broke the outright lap record. Then he won the 1300 cc final at Cadwell Park. The highlight of the season for him must have been his tremendous first F1 win at Mallory Park; during which he set a new outright lap record of 50.5 seconds, knocking almost a second off the previous record set by the reigning sidecar world champions Steve Webster and Tony Hewitt. The 'King of Cadwell' title was added to the success list when Trevor Nation won the 1300 cc final at Cadwell Park on October 1. He went on to compound that success by winning this F1 race the next day, during which he set a sensational new outright solo lap record of 1 minute 33.7 seconds. Both Trevor Nation and the Norton rotary had found form and were delighting the race fans both at the circuits and those watching at home.

By this time Simon Buckmaster had lost confidence in the rotary racer because of the handling problems that he was still experiencing. In October, just before the Power Bike International Meeting at Brands Hatch, he decided to leave the team. The team were very careful in choosing a replacement and studied the form of a number of riders before making a choice. The rider that Brian approached was up-and-coming star, Steve Spray. When he phoned Steve with the invitation to race the rotary racer at the Power Bike International Meeting, Brian did say to Steve that he should bring his own race bike to the meeting just in case he didn't get on with the rotary. On the day Steve put in an extraordinary performance, winning both the Power Bike International race and the final round of the British Formula One series; all the more remarkable when you consider the short time that he had actually ridden the machine. Summing up his effort Steve said, 'As soon as I rode the Norton I knew that it was a winner.'

Watching this impressive display among the crowds that day at Brands Hatch were representatives from a prospective sponsor: they liked what they saw on the track and also the enthusiastic reaction of the crowd. . .

October was a good month for the Norton team, with Trevor's success and newcomer Steve Spray's superb outing at Brands Hatch. The FIM had finally come to a decision as to whether the Norton rotary should be allowed into the Formula One Championship. The FIM congress voted to rate the Norton claimed 588 cc rotary engine at 1.7:1, which classified it as 999 cc, eligible for entry into the prestigious World Formula One Championship. The classification would last for one season only and be subject to review if the machine proved too fast.

JPS returns

The winter months saw a great deal of work put into the machines and a lot of time was spent on looking for a suitable sponsor for the racing venture. Road racing is a notoriously expensive business and many a talented

Steve Spray on the RCW588 won two races on his debut at Brands Hatch (Picture *Motor Cycle News*).

team has foundered through lack of cash. It was therefore a great boost to team morale when Norton announced their intention of returning to international class racing supported by a three-year sponsorship deal signed with their old acquaintances Imperial Tobacco. The sum involved was rumoured to be around half a million pounds. As before, the team would race under the John Player banner which had last appeared on Peter Williams Commando-based racer with which he won the Isle of Man Formula 750 TT back in 1973.

The John Player Special/Norton race team was officially launched with a big champagne reception held at the Inter-Continental Hotel in London in February, during which the race replica road bike, the P55 (which had already been shown at Earls Court in the Autumn) was unveiled in its new colours. When it first appeared the machine had been totally dark grey with red wheels but it was now in impressive JPS livery of black, grey and gold, like the race machines.

With the John Player sponsorship, Brian Crighton could move his race team into a purpose-built 5,000-square-foot race and development department. Money also meant that work could continue on experiments with a liquid cooled engine for the race machines. Liquid cooling would actually reduce the weight of the engine as it would mean that the finning around the engine would be unnecessary; even with the addition of a water jacket, radiator, and other ancillaries, it would weigh less.

The John Player involvement meant that a more professional approach was required for the team presentation and organisation. That is not to say that the effort made by Brian Crighton and his team was not professional; but in addition to racing, Brian was still carrying out development work at the factory. To meet the demands of the new team profile it was decided that a professional team manager was needed, which led to the appointment of Nick Colliss. As team manager he would be responsible for the organisation and running of the team, all its members, transport, accommodation and all racing activity at the tracks, a very demanding job that requires exceptional organisational skills.

At the start of the season the new water-cooled machines were released and in addition to their new engines they featured an improved chassis, mono-shock rear suspension and an electronic engine management system. With water-cooling new fairings also had to be made. These were similar to those used on the Yamaha YZR500 GP machines with large vertical vents at each side to direct cooling air on to the radiators.

The 1989 season started well for the John Player Special Norton men in black at the Euro-lantic meeting at Donington Park, where Trevor won his first race on the new water-cooled twin rear-shock machine. Steve Spray took second place. But despite the one-two finish, it was obvious to the enthusiastic Norton supporters that both riders were having handling problems as the

JPS NORTON RCW588 TECHNICAL SPECIFICATIONS

Engine:	Liquid cooled twin-rotor rotary.
Displacement:	588cc
Compression ratio:	9.2:1
Carburation:	Twin Amal Smoothbores
Ignition:	Norton "hall effect" triggered capacitor discharge
Gearbox:	5 speed, constant mesh
Clutch:	20-plate "wet" clutch using sintered bronze friction plates and diaphragm spring
Power output:	More than 135bhp at 9,800 rpm at shaft
Maximum torque:	77lbs/ft at 8,000 rpm
Frame:	Spondon twin spar aluminium
Brakes:	Twin 310mm front discs with four-piston 1 piece Lockheed calipers
	Single 210mm rear disc with twin-piston Brembo caliper
Wheels:	3.5 x 17 three-spoke magnesium P.V.M front wheel
	5.75 x 17 three-spoke magnesium P.V.M rear wheel
Tyres:	Michelin radials
Weight:	Less than 145kgs

ABOVE An ROO45 A10 surface discharge spark plug as used by the team (Picture G W Aldridge).

ABOVE RIGHT Dave Hickman at work at the Norton race base.

RIGHT Trevor Nation and Steve Spray at Donington. Whilst racing, there are no 'team orders': both riders are out there to win.

machines squirmed their way to the front.

The season had started well for the new race team but it quickly became apparent that the team, despite having a team manager, was not working as a team but had become fragmented. Each rider had his own transporter and more often than not in the paddock the two, 'team' riders set up camp separately. The importance of a good back-up team cannot be over-emphasised. A good mechanic can make a mediocre

rider good and a poor mechanic can relegate the best rider to last. Nowadays the back room personnel are more technicians than just mechanics.

Steve's machines were prepared by Dave Evans and Ray 'Ronnie' Corbett. Each rider used two machines both of which were prepared prior to the race, one of which can be used as a spare if anything goes wrong just before the race starts. 'I look after the engine and the gearbox while Ray sorts out the carburation, suspension, tyres and other ancillaries. Ray and myself have worked together, on and off for twenty years and by putting our skills together I think we make a good team.' Trevor's machines were looked after by Chris Clarke and Gordon Jeakins with additional help from apprentice Paul Vince, Brian Crighton and Dave Hickman who gave help wherever needed but concentrated on the development projects.

May was a busy month for the team as Trevor went off to Japan with Brian Crighton, Dave Hickman and Chris Clarke, to contest the World Formula One Championship at Sugo. Steve stayed to take part in the North-West 200 race in Ireland and the televised Shell Oils Formula One round at Donington Park. It should be remembered that publicity for the sponsors is a major priority for team financial survival. Norton were looking for their first win at the NW200 for 23 years and over 70,000 were expecting a good result. Their hopes appeared to be fulfilled when Steve took the lead early on, but in the slippery conditions over the drying course he eventually lost out.

At Donington Steve was partnered by road circuit specialist Steve Cull who had been invited into the team to race Trevor's spare machine. In the Formula One race watched by thousands at the track and millions at home watching Sunday afternoon TV, Steve Spray put the JPS Norton in the limelight at the start. But by halfway the pressure was telling on the tyres and he lost places to Roger Burnett and Terry Rymer forcing him to finish in third place. His team mate Steve Cull had not faired so well, forced to retire on lap seven with a broken gearbox.

The 1989 JPS Norton race team, left to right: Ray Corbett, Steve Spray, Dave Evans, Dave Hickman, Brian Crighton, Gordon Jenkins, Trevor Nation, Chris Clarke.

The men in black, Donington. For 1990, the Dunlop tyres were replaced by 17-in Michelin radials and the fairing was modified; compare the 1989 machine (OPPOSITE). In the TT F1, Trevor Nation (BELOW) was second, Steve Spray (LEFT) was third.

In Japan, Trevor had good practice sessions on the new water-cooled machine but protests were lodged from several of the opposition who argued that the machine had not been properly homologated and was therefore not eligible to race. Trevor therefore had to switch to his old air-cooled machine and was slower and only qualified in fourteenth place. At the start of the race a mechanical problem struck and in frustration Trevor turned into the exit of the pit lane to try and get to his pit. In doing so he earned immediate disqualification.

Later the same month the first big breakthrough came for team newcomer Steve Spray at the first British Formula One Championship race at Mallory Park in Leicestershire. Having made his usual good start, Steve had to fight hard to stay in front of the Yamaha ridden by World Superbike Championship contender Terry Rymer. This performance had the Norton sliding and wriggling but it provided excellent entertainment for the fans. The race was held in front of a record crowd, many of whom were obviously there to see the Norton put down a challenge.

This performance was followed by further successes in the championship series, four wins from the first five races of the eight-round championship. Steve Spray was the man to watch and a growing number of people were fascinated by the Shell Oils Supercup series that was televised. The support from the fans is important to any rider and can be a valuable spur to performance, as Steve Spray explains: 'Everywhere we went the crowds were right behind us and that really did help. British race fans have not had much home-brewed success to cheer about, and it seemed that they were as hungry as we were for the JPS Norton to win.' With all this support Steve responded brilliantly.

Attention then turned to the Isle of Man TT, the high spot of the British motorcycle racing calendar and the fans were expecting a lot after Steve Spray's earlier performances. The stage was set for the Nortons to dominate the Senior race, with Trevor partnered by Steve Cull, but it was not to be. Much to his embarrassment, Trevor crashed only ten feet from the start; re-starting, he only got as far as the mountain before running out of petrol. Steve Cull didn't fare much better, as he was faced with gearbox problems and had to push home in 23rd place.

After such bitter disappointment in the Isle of Man the team set off for Donington and the next round of the British Formula One Championship. Things could only get better! According to race team manager Nick Colliss, everyone knew that the team was having problems. Steve was on form but Trevor was having more than his fair shair of bad luck. According to Nick the team were working on these problems. Steve had

Steve Cull in action. He gained third place at the Ulster GP.

decided to race his second machine in the Formula One race as it had a slightly longer wheelbase and different carburation that seemed to suit the East Midlands circuit. His decision was correct: and he stormed away at the start and finished three seconds ahead of Carl Fogarty and Jamie Whitham, with Trevor in fourth place. During the race Steve broke the outright lap record set by Freddie Spencer back in 1984. In the second race, the King of Donington, the race had to be re-started after a crash. Although Steve was in front in the second part, he lost the title to Carl Fogarty on aggregate by one fifth of a second. Team mate Trevor had been delayed getting out for the second practice session and was forced to start from the back of the grid, then he had to retire when his water pump failed.

From this chapter of accidents it was patently clear that all in the Norton camp was not well; there were too many recurring problems with machine reliability, breakdowns due to minor faults were too common. These were often caused by poor race preparation. Several times throttle cables broke, resulting in machines not finishing. The cause was that the throttle cable followed a tortuous route around the outside of the frame and under race stresses it sometimes frayed and broke.

On the way to the next Formula One round at Assen in Holland, the team went via Belgium and were kept waiting at customs for half a day. This delay was not going to deter the team from its race preparation. As Ray Corbett recalls, 'We just got the bikes out of the van, stripped them down and prepared them for the race there and then. In the end we had quite a large crowd watching us work.' Trevor scored a tenth place at Assen but had only managed to complete two out of the six meetings of the series.

Action then moved to Cadwell Park where Steve finished fourth but Trevor crashed out on the fourth lap and injured his hand. This put him out for the next round at Knockhill in Scotland so his machine was offered to Ray Stringer. At the Scottish circuit Steve, who had won each round so far in the series, took third place while Ray Stringer crashed out at the chicane. Then at Snetterton the Nortons found their form and Steve and Ray fought their way to first and second in the two races; but they both had to fight the machine through the corners and make up ground on the long Revett straight. By winning at Snetterton, Steve set a new outright lap record and extended his lead in the Formula One Championship to 27 points. At the next round at Donington Park Steve finished third but

Trevor retired early. The next day, both Nortons retired after only a few laps.

At the Ulster GP, Steve Cull gave Norton their best result in the World Championships with third place. Trevor's machine expired early in the race with an ignition problem, and in the next race his exhaust ejector system packed up.

It was obvious that the Norton race team was finding trouble in organising itself and that the man who was going to take the blame for this was the race team manager, Nick Colliss. Rumours now began to spread about his replacement, one candidate being Roger Marshall, who had retired from road racing the year before. He had tried the rotary at a test session at Cadwell Park. The team needed to be re-structured in an effort to regain the impetus with which they had begun. One of the main concerns was for future sponsorship, and so Bob Rowley was drafted in to supervise action within the team for the rest of the season. This helped to allay Trevor Nation's growing fear that Steve's machines were receiving preferential treatment.

These rumours seemed to have an effect on the riders: at Thruxton on August 20 Steve charged to another win, but at Donington the following week it was Trevor who took the honours. For the first time since the Eurolantic meeting at Easter, Trevor Nation gained the upper hand in the TT Superbike race, having had to fight Steve all the way until the latter tried too hard at Goddard and fell for the first time that year.

Hopes were high for the race of the year at Mallory Park and it was a close-run thing with the two Nortons hounding eventual winner Terry Rymer. Trevor was beaten by a wheel and Steve (who could have won the Championship with second place) sensibly decided to take third place rather than push too hard.

First title

In the televised Shell oils Super Cup Formula One race at Brands Hatch the Nortons were again explosive, (almost literally, as Trevor's bike had a belly pan fire in the pit lane during practice). Undeterred and on the same machine he went out to take second place with Steve following a safe fourth to win the Super Cup series, the first title for the new RCW588. The machine now had the engine located an inch lower in the frame. Additional changes had also been made to the suspension and these modifications were obviously working.

At Cadwell Park Steve Spray finished in second place to give Norton their first British Championship since 1973, the MCN Formula One crown. Having only been a Norton rider since the previous October when he won two races as a stand-in for Simon Buckmaster, it had taken him eleven months to win the two championships. The fans that were delighted with this success were treated to a further display when Steve won the King of Cadwell race, so taking the title from his team mate who had won it the year before. The rest of the season was academic, although it did not stop the effort: at Donington Steve took fourth place in the Superbike race and a third place in the Formula One round.

ABOVE LEFT **Trevor Nation points out a few things to race manager Nick Colliss. (Picture** *Motor Cycle News*).

RIGHT **Trevor Nation winning the Donington TT Superbike Championship race – his first win since Easter.**

1989 FORMULA ONE BRITISH CHAMPIONSHIP FINAL POSITIONS

	Rider	Machine	MP	DP	KH	SN	CP	CP	DP	BH	Total
1	S Spray	JPS Norton	15	15	10	15	15	12	10	12	104
2	T Rymer	Loctite Yamaha	12	0	15	6	0	10	8	15	66
3	C Fogarty	Honda	6	12	0	0	0	15	15	0	48
4	J Whitham	Durex Suzuki	0	10	12	8	12	0	0	0	42
5	S Chambers	Honda	8	5	0	10	0	6	3	0	32
6	M Phillips	Loctite Yamaha	0	4	8	5	0	5	1	8	31
7	S Hislop	Honda	0	6	0	0	0	8	6	4	24
8	T Nation	JPS Norton	0	8	0	0	8	0	0	6	22
9	R Stringer	Yamaha/JPS Norton*	5	3	0	12*	0	0	0	0	20
10	S Manley	Yamaha	0	2	0	4	6	4	0	2	18

1989 SHELL OILS SUPERCUP FINAL POSITIONS

	Name	Machine	DP	CP	Th	MP	BH	Total
1	Steve Spray	JPS Norton	8	8	10	8	7	41
2	Terry Rymer	Loctite Yamaha	9	0	0	10	8	27
3	Carl Fogarty	Honda	0	10	7	7	0	24
4	Trevor Nation	JPS Norton	0	0	5	9	9	23
	Brian Morrison	Honda	3	6	8	6	0	23
6	Steve Chambers	Honda	5	5	6	0	5	21
7	Mark Phillips	Loctite Yamaha	4	0	1	5	10	20
8	Roger Burnett	Honda	10	7	0	2	0	19
9	Steve Hislop	Honda	7	0	4	0	6	17
10	Ray Stringer	Yamaha	1	0	9	0	0	10

ABOVE Very agreeable reading at the end of the 1989, for the team – and for its sponsor.

Steve Spray duels with Terry Rymer at the Powerbike International, Brands Hatch (Picture *Motor Cycle News*).

As a finale to the season Steve saved plenty of action for the Brands Powerbike International where he had first raced a Norton so spectacularly only twelve months earlier. There was an epic start-to-finish battle between Steve Spray and Terry Rymer, in both the Powerbike race and the Formula One race. During the F1 battle the two riders pushed each other hard to drop the circuit lap record to 47.6 seconds, Terry Rymer just managed to beat his rival by a tenth of a second. (Trevor, who was still recovering from rib and hand injuries managed to fight his painful way up to third place.) In the Superbike race, the two riders again shot off with Terry just in the lead and Steve looking for a way past. When he got his wheel in front going into Paddock, the stands erupted with cheers, but groaned as Rymer shut him out on the exit. Several laps later he tried the same manoeuvre with no success. Eventually, Steve managed to control the viciously squirming machine as he powered hard round the outside coming out of Clearways to take the lead and win, providing the Norton supporters with a superb end to the season.

The question of a new team manager had still not been settled. After careful consideration and in consultation with the sponsors, it was decided in October that the best move would be to bring in a more experienced manager. This prompted an approach to former Honda race team manager Barry Symmons who was then circuit manager of Snetterton race circuit. After careful consideration of the offer Barry accepted and agreed to take up the post by that coming December. When he took the job it was done so on the understanding that certain personnel with whom he had worked before would also be given a position in his team formation: namely Dave Hickman, Ron Williams the chassis expert and Chris Mehew, who had worked with Ron Haslam as mechanic/engineer in the Elf GP team.

In early November, Ron Williams attended a testing session held at Donington Park when Grand Prix rider Niall Mackenzie had a one-lap ride on a twin-shock machine. This session was very short, because of thick fog blanketing the circuit; but from one lap Niall Mackenzie cast doubts on the machine's twin-shock rear suspension. With Ron's presence at this session, plus Brian's application of a new suspension monitoring device, speculation grew over possible chassis and suspension changes for the new season. The following month, Norton again asked Niall Mackenzie to test the new twin shock at Donington. This time the session allowed him to put plenty of laps in and he experienced a very favourable impression of the whole machine, including the twin-shock rear end.

Upon taking up the job of team manager Barry quickly began to re-organise the team, from the ground up. His first move was to turn the race team headquarters into a more efficient unit that was as self-supportive as possible.

Plans for the 1990 season were announced at a champagne reception at the RAC club in London held by Imperial Tobacco, where their sponsorship consultant Peter Dyke said that JPS had been delighted with the team's 1989 success. 'With two major championship wins under our belts, JPS Norton can look forward to even greater successes in the 1990 season,' he said. 'The team's achievements in coming from nowhere to win the British Formula One and Supercup Championships in such a short time has been remarkable. Riders Steve Spray and Trevor Nation have done a great job throughout the season and have worked hard to put JPS Norton on top. The great British public has been right behind us all the way and JPS is proud to have been involved with the resurgence of the legendary Norton name. We are confident that JPS Norton can now gear up to match the success we have had in Britain with an equally impressive performance on the world stage.'

Niall Mackenzie with Brian Crighton, Steve Spray and Trevor Nation at Donington Park (Picture *Motor Cycle News*).

ABOVE LEFT Brian Crighton's suspension data gathering system. (Picture *Motor Cycle News*).

LEFT Peter Dyke, the sponsorship consultant. Peter was the man who recognised the potential of the Norton as powerful advertising and secured the financial backing of Imperial Tobacco (JPS).

1990

For the 1990 season Steve Spray had secured his place with his brilliant performance throughout the season but Trevor's seemed less secure, although at the end of the season it was announced that the factory had, 'an understanding with Trevor'! At the same time it was widely reported in the motorcycle press that approaches had been made to double F1 champion Carl Fogarty to secure his services for the coming season. According to a report in *Motor Cycle News*, 17 January 1990, Carl Fogarty was quoted as saying, 'They [Norton] have laid a contract on the table for me to sign, I'm considering this year's deal hard, but what really interests me is their Grand Prix and Superbike plans.' Unfortunately for Carl, the meeting to decide the future for the rotary in Grand Prix was not until March and he would have to make a decision before this. With such an uncertain situation, Carl decided to stay with Honda.

'The Management', left to right: Barry Symmons, Chris Mehew, Ron Williams.

Barry Symmons

From school Barry Symmons went to an agricultural college near Guildford to train as a farm manager, until a neck injury forced him to leave. He then took a job with the Milk Marketing Board. At the weekends he was helping to run a sidecar at meetings all over the country. Rex White, team manager for Suzuki, recognized Barry's talent for organisation and offered him a job as his assistant. In 1978, the Honda team approached Barry and offered him the job of race team manager which he held from 1978 until 1987.

When the Honda team reduced its budget for racing, Barry decided to leave and try something else. He became circuit manager of Snetterton race circuit until he was approached by Norton. He was offered the job as race team manager and accepted but only started the job in December 1989. He immediately began re-organising the team. 'It is my job to see that the riders are happy;' obviously if the riders are happy they can perform to the best of their ability. The same thing can be said of the mechanics. 'The mechanics in my opinion are almost as important as the riders, so also need to be well looked after.'

The Norton JPS team certainly became much better organised and presented a very highly polished appearance wherever they went. Since his arrival at Norton the machines certainly became more reliable.

The responsibilities of a team manager are incredibly varied, on race day Barry becomes totally engrossed with the varied demands of his team and allows nothing to interfere with his train of thought. But, if they win, he has been known to smile!

It was announced that for the 1990 season the JPS Norton team would enter two of the water-cooled rotaries in all five races of the International Formula One Cup series that would begin in Japan on May 13 at the Sugo circuit. Races would then follow at the Isle of Man TT, moving on to Portugal, Finland and then finally to Dundrod. The series would be contested by Trevor Nation and Robert Dunlop, the brother of Joey Dunlop, the highly successful TT and superbike rider. On the home front, the team would focus on the high profile Shell/Motor Cycle News F1 Supercup and MCN's TT Superbike series which would both be televised. In addition, the longer term plan was to enter World Superbike and the ultimate aim was entry into the Grand Prix, subject to acceptance by the FIM for the 1991 season. The FIM's annual general meeting in March would determine whether the rotary engine would be allowed into the Grand Prix races and also give a ruling on the capacity of the engine.

By February, team plans were finalised and the first testing session for both riders and mechanics was held at Snetterton. Usually at that time of the year the circuit is bitterly cold, with winds sweeping in off the North Sea and often wet, but that month produced some freak sunshine and warmth. The dry sunny day seemed to be a good sign for the team and the riders, Steve Spray and Trevor Nation both put in fast lap times on the revamped circuit. In fact, both riders were lapping the circuit within nine seconds of the 1 minute 6.9 seconds lap record time that Steve had set the previous year, despite change to the circuit with the introduction of a restriction at the entrance of Russell's that almost makes it a chicane, the purpose being to slow competitors.

The improvements at the circuit had been implemented by Barry Symmons the year before when he was the manager of the Norfolk circuit and he believed that the lap times set by his riders would fall even lower. Impressive lap times by both riders were partially attributed to the changes in tyres that Barry Symmons had decided upon during the off season.

For the previous three years the Nortons had been using Dunlop tyres with which both riders were happy, but there had been quality control problems with the tyres towards the end of the season. Even the Grand Prix riders such as Wayne Rainey had experienced problems with the Dunlop tyres. In practice, the tyres performed very well for the early laps but their performance had a tendency suddenly to drop off, especially in the latter stages when riders demanded more from them. Therefore it was decided that the team would use Michelins. A deal was made for both tyres and technical support in exchange for tyre performance data and technical data. A concession was made by the tyre manufacturers, who agreed to the 'Michelin Man' logo being picked out in gold so that it matched the JPS Norton livery. For the 1990 season Michelin would make available $18/67 \times 17$-in radials with a choice of two compounds, the 1223 and the 1423. The 1223 compound was a well proven compound but the 1423 mixture was a relatively new compound, yet fully endorsed by Eddie Lawson.

A rider's trust in the performance of the tyres is important and it was generally felt that Michelins and Dunlops behave differently. The Michelin's were very grippy but when they lost adhesion they did so with very little warning to the rider. The Dunlops that Trevor and Steve were used to, were more prone to sliding but they gave plenty of feel to the rider. In the words of the race team manager, 'We chose Michelin tyres because of their excellent race record and their sheer consistency in all conditions on any type of circuit.' As the lap times at Snetterton showed, both Steve and Trevor were delighted with the new tyres, according to Steve, 'The bike seems to be more stable at high speed, it flicks into corners more easily yet it doesn't slide.'

Not all these improvements were the result of a tyre change. Changes had also been made to the chassis by Ron Williams, widely regarded in racing circles as one of the best chassis engineers in the business, who had joined the team at the same time as Barry Symmons with whom he had worked before for the Honda Britain team. Barry had decided that he wanted to make as few changes as necessary to the machines before the start of the season, as he wanted to make his own assessment of their performance. So during the winter Ron had only tinkered, improving the existing machines specifications by, for example, modifying the swinging arm pivot that had had an annoying habit of sticking after the first few laps. Engine heat had caused the swinging arm pivot to expand, so a change of materials was used to cure it. The rear suspension linkage was also given attention to smooth its action. Changes were also made to the brakes: instead of using Spondon discs, they decided to use those from PVM. The calipers remained as AP-Lockheed units but the more expensive one-piece units were fitted. Minor changes were made to reduce mechanical failure and speed components replacement, and to improve the image of the machines. The routing of the throttle cables which had caused a number of DNFs the previous season was now put more freely through the frame. The torque arm was modified to prevent it from fouling the silencer when the ride height was altered. To help the race mechanics, the tensioning of the rear chain was made more simple. On the old machines it had involved removing three nuts from the swinging arm, now only one.

For 1990, Steve kept his two mechanics, Dave Evans and Ray Corbett, who had worked so well for him during the previous season; Trevor had lost his mechanic Pete Spinks who returned to the factory. Chris Clarke had already left the team after Assen and Gordon Jeakins also left. So for the new season Trevor had two new mechanics, Chris Pike and Malcolm Heath. Malcolm had moved from test and development rider to racer, and then race mechanic. Chris Mehew, who had worked with Ron Haslam at ELF, the French racing team, had also been drafted into the team as Chief Technician. His skills were well know to Barry Symmons with whom he had worked before.

To improve the team image and also to aid efficiency the whole procedure for team organisation at race meetings was carefully re-organised by Barry Symmons. Instead of having separate vans for the riders' machines the new procedure was that all four machines would be taken in one of the distinctive liveried Mercedes vans and all the tools and other equipment

ABOVE Trevor Nation with mechanics Malcolm Heath and Chris Pike.

ABOVE LEFT Pre-race preparation. Ray Corbett prepares Steve's machine while former Norton racer Malcolm Heath prepares Trevor's.

LEFT Steve Spray attended by mechanics Dave Evans and Ray (Ronnie) Corbett.

would be taken in the other. At the circuit, the vans would park next to each other and a special tent be fixed between them, providing a large work space. Every member of the support team had a specific job to do on arrival so that the 'unit' was ready to go into action straight away. Air temperature, air density and the latest weather forecasts are vital information that has to be continually monitored by all race teams, as they will effect the preparation and setting of the carburettors. Each machine was prepared by the rider's individual pair of mechanics, but inter-action between them is paramount to ensure a successful performance at each meeting. To record the preparations a check list was (and is) kept for each machine.

The riders make their own way to the circuits in this

country. Each has a caravan in which they can relax before and after racing. They always make time for the fans, whatever the problems they are contending with. Usually the team travels to the circuit a day or so before the actual meeting and stays at a nearby hotel, where they can eat and sleep comfortably: they are of no use unless they are on top form. Early on the day of the race they leave the hotel and travel to the circuit in the team bus and set everything out that they need. After scrutineering, where the machines are checked to see that they are safe and comply with all the rules, the riders sign on, and their clothing and helmet are also checked. The machines are then fuelled ready for practice.

As soon as the rider takes his machine, the spare machine is started. The riders then go out for practice and their mechanics take the spare machine up to the pit area with a range of tools for minor adjustments. After practice the machines are returned to the paddock area and are stripped so that any adjustments can be made before they are again made ready, this time to race.

Barry Symmons decided that the cosmetics of the machines needed some attention, which resulted in a new seat/tail unit and a new fairing. This owed its origins to a Honda NSR500 fairing he had acquired.

Norton Racing

Rider _____	Machine _____
Frame No _____	Engine No _____
Name of Race _____	Date _____
Circuit _____	Distance _____ km
Air Pressure _____ Temp _____	Humidity _____ %

FRONT FORK		GEARS RATIO SPEED (km/hr)
Offset _____		1st _____
Through _____		2nd _____
Spring _____		3rd _____
Pre-load _____		4th _____
Comp Force _____		5th _____
Reb Force _____		6th _____
Oil _____ SAE _____		Primary Ratio _____ x _____
Oil Level _____		Final Ratio _____ x _____
Brake Pad F _____		REAR UNIT
R _____		Type _____
CARBURETTOR		Spring _____
Type _____		Pre-load _____
MJ _____		Comp Force _____
JN _____		Reb Force _____
HT _____		Ride Height _____ mm
PJ _____		Tyre Make _____
AS _____		Front _____
		Rear _____
Spark Plug _____		Race Distance _____ km
Fuel Consumption _____ km/ltr		Fastest Lap _____

REMARKS

ABOVE **The race workshop at Lichfield (Photo Chris Mehew).**

LEFT **Racing checklist. A record of all adjustments and settings of each machine is maintained as a check for mechanics and general source of reference.**

The new fairing had been altered a great deal to fit the rotary. It had been made as aerodynamically slippery as possible, a major factor considering the speeds that these machines are capable of attaining. It is amazing how slim and physically small these machines actually are in comparison to other race machines,; in fact, it is possible to fit the fairing of, say, a Yamaha OWO1-one of Norton's main rivals – over that of the RCW588.

After a highly successful open test session at Snetterton both riders were delighted with the performance of their machines and the new tyres, although Steve, who had returned marginally faster times, was still concerned that he had not been able to establish the breakaway point on the Michelin's. Trevor on the other hand was, quote, 'as happy as a pig in manure'.

The JPS Norton race team set off for the first race of the season at Cadwell Park on March 11 in high spirits. At Cadwell in the TT F1 and Production races, Steve rode a brilliant race to first place, hotly pursued by Trevor in second place; a result they repeated in the second race.

At Brands Hatch on April 13, Trevor and Steve qualified in first and second place with Steve only 1/10th of a second behind his team mate. Trevor actually won the race and Steve had to content himself with fifth place and the fastest lap. Donington Park was the venue for the next race, where Steve came second and Trevor took third place in the TT F1/Superbike race. In the second race of the meeting it was Trevor who won laurels, beating Steve into second place. These positions were reversed at Castle Coombe on April 28. The following day at Thruxton Trevor won the F1 race, but Steve came off in a spectacular way in the same race at over 140 mph and injured his left wrist. Afterwards inspection of his Manx Kushitani team leathers revealed that there was very little damage to them. In fact, the makers only had to replace some of the badges for the leathers to be as good as new.

Prior to the North West 200 race, the machines were given new fairings specially designed for the Isle of Man with the aim of reducing wind resistance. According to Barry Symmons, 'We had been taking a long hard look at the aerodynamics of the machine and knew there were some improvements which could be made. There were several different solutions which were tried before we arrived at the final design.' The new fairings arrived at the race team headquarters at Lichfield only two days before the team was due to leave for Northern Ireland. After they were fitted, a machine was taken to Brunting-thorpe airfield where it was given a brief try-out that confirmed its high speed potential. Both riders also gave the thumbs up to the new style fairing, The bike already looked great but this fairing makes it look even better,' said Robert Dunlop.

For the North West 200 race on May 19 held on closed public roads that link the Causeway coast towns of Portstewart, Coleraine and Portrush (a distance of 8.9 miles) Trevor Nation qualified in first place and Robert Dunlop in second place. Both riders felt that the new fairing was working well aerodynamically, and in practice Robert went through the speed trap at over 189 mph. In the race itself, Robert won the supporting Superbike race and in doing so set a new lap record. (Robert also won the 125 race on a Honda). Trevor was forced to retire with gearbox trouble in the first race and again in the second with a fuel problem. After the race, team manager Barry Symmons was amazed by the reaction of the crowd. 'There were old guys with tears in their eyes and the whole crowd were on their feet cheering. It was a fantastic atmosphere. 'I felt really sorry for Robert who had to rush away almost immediately to get to the next day's British Championship event at Snetterton and was hardly able to savour his big moment.' The North West 200 is considered by many people to be a good work-out for riders and

The change to Michelin rubber was approved of by the riders.

machines before the Isle of Man TT; Barry Symmons must have been a happy man.

The following day, the Norton race team were at Snetterton where during practice Trevor Nation fell, suffering concussion and badly bruised ribs that side-lined him from the race. But honour was upheld by Steve Spray. The race had to be re-started after Simon Beck fell at Riches and an ambulance had to be brought onto the circuit. When the race was re-started Steve chased Terry Rymer and Carl Fogarty, managed to split them and then take the lead on lap three. Both Terry Rymer and Jim Whitham fought Steve for the lead but despite his heavily strapped left wrist he beat them off to win. During the race Steve obviously concentrated on his riding but after he had won it was very obvious that the wrist was causing him some pain. 'My wrist is really stiff and sore now, but during the race I didn't feel a thing.' Steve was also impressed with the new style fairing: 'The bike not only looks great it goes like a rocket, I'm sure that Trevor and Robert will do a great job at the TT and I wish them the best of luck.'

The win at Snetterton was watched by a huge crowd eager for the Norton's to beat the Japanese opposition and, more significantly, by millions of BBC television viewers who must have enjoyed the hard-fought tussle. Many of the fans had also wanted to see Robert Dunlop do a lap of honour after his wins in the North West 200 but this was vetoed by race officials; (Barry Symmons took the blame for this).

During the following week Steve and Trevor were busy with another aspect of their team responsibilities

ABOVE The slimline new fairing for 1990.

LEFT Steve Spray, full of the joys of spring but not competing in the Isle of Man TT in 1990. The 1990 season was an unlucky one for Steve, and his last in Norton colours.

RIGHT Trevor Nation on the winner's rostrum; a smile for the cameras despite the pain from injured ribs.

public relations. Both riders took great pleasure in handing over the first F1 road bike to the winner of a lottery. Lucky man!

Following the success at Snetterton, the Norton race team packed up and headed for the Isle of Man TT races where it was hoped that double TT winner Trevor and the 1989 125 cc TT winner Robert Dunlop would take the honours. The aim was to score Norton's first TT victory since 1973, when Peter Williams won the formula 750 race from Mick Grant, both on John Player-sponsored Nortons. Both Trevor, (who is extremely patriotic) and Robert believed that they could put a British-built machine back into the TT winners circle.

Trevor had raced successfully at the Isle of Man before; in 1984 he had won the 750 Production TT and in 1986 won the 1000 cc Production TT and for 1990 was evidently looking forward to racing on the island. 'I have never been so confident before a TT campaign. Everything is coming together brilliantly and I know we

are going to have a great TT. It has always been my ambition to win one of the big TT races and I want to score that win on a JPS Norton.' So keen was he that he actually went to the island some weeks before the TT to videotape all the resurfaced sections of the circuit and learn the sections that had been altered or that had caused him problems the year before.

Trevor's team mate at the TT was Robert Dunlop, nicknamed the 'Matchstick Man' by the Norton team, who won the Manx Grand Prix Newcomers race on the Mountain Circuit in 1983 and went on to contest his first TT race in 1984. He began his race preparations early by arriving on the island days before so that he could refresh his memory of the circuit. 'I am treating the TT very seriously this year so I decided to arrive early and spend time concentrating on the sections of the circuit that have given me trouble in the past. I reckon the JPS Norton is the fastest bike I have ever ridden and it's clear that its full potential has yet to be realised on the Isle of Man. I am out to change that this year.'

The JPS Norton team were entered in two six-lap races, the Formula One TT and the Senior TT. In official practice for the first race Robert managed to secure third place with a time of 18.54.40 and Trevor was placed 12th with 19.30.00, not as good as they had hoped. In the actual Formula 1 race, Robert Dunlop finished in third place and gained fifteen points toward the World F1 cup Championship; Trevor finished 6th which gave him ten points. During the race Trevor had

a nasty shock when on his last lap a strong gust of wind shot him off the track. He smashed through some posts and went down a grassy slope. He managed somehow to stay on and rode the machine moto-cross style back onto the circuit, where he continued with a gaping hole in the fairing, a smashed screen and plenty of grass and mud. In the Senior race Trevor, who was in a great deal of pain from his tumble at Snetterton compounded by his excursion off the circuit in the F1 race, pushed himself to the limit to achieve a well earned second place, with Robert having to retire on the fourth lap.

Norton created an interest in the paddock from a very particular source. Visiting the Isle of Man to watch the racing was Honda four stroke boss Hideo Tanaka, who visited the Norton camp to inspect one of the rotary racers – under the wary eye of Barry Symmons.

On Monday June 11 Barry Symmons announced that Trevor Nation would not be contesting the next round of the F1 World Championship at Vila Real in Portugal. The sponsors preferred him and Steve Spray to appear at the televised Pembrey meeting, the sole Norton challenge in Portugal would come from Robert Dunlop.

The team returned to the mainland to appear at the post-TT meeting at Donington Park on June 17; both riders were keen to return to form. In practice for the MCN TT Superbike race, Trevor claimed 6th place whilst Steve could only manage 14th place. In the race itself Steve came 4th and Trevor 5th. In the second race, Steve came 3rd and Trevor 4th. These positions were further improved in the TT F1 race where Trevor came 2nd followed by Steve who in 3rd place had actually set a new lap record. Cadwell Park the following weekend saw Trevor repeat his second place finish behind Terry Rymer and Steve relegated to fifth.

At Pembrey in Wales, (important to JPS because it was televised) in race one Steve came third and Trevor fifth. In the second race, it all came together: Steve was first, hotly pursued across the line by Trevor in second place. The same day, over 1500 km to the south in the blazing sunshine of Portugal, Robert Dunlop finished a creditable second place to Honda-mounted Carl Fogarty in the Vila Real round of the World Championship, giving him another 17 points that took his total to 32. The series leader after the first two rounds was Fogarty on forty points for two outright wins. The JPS Norton team were doing very well against some very fierce competition.

The Pembrey meeting was also interesting in that it saw the racing debut of the Norton rotary powered sidecar outfit of Colin Rust and his World Champion passenger Tony Hewitt, formerly partner to Steve Webster. On the Sunday the black liveried outfit that still lacked sponsorship powered its way to fifth place in front of an intrigued crowd.

Fortunes took a nosedive on July 7, when Steve and Trevor ventured north of the border to the Knockhill circuit tucked away in the hills near Dunfermline in Scotland, where in the Shell Oils Supercup TT F1 race Steve came eighth and Trevor finished tenth.

Returning south to Snetterton for the two-day sun-kissed meeting, on July 14 and 15, both riders were very determined to return to form. In the fourth round MCN TT Superbike race Trevor won but Steve did not finish. The next day, in the round five race, Trevor came first and Steve came second. Trevor and Steve were obviously firing on all cylinders (hardly an appropriate metaphor) and in the Race of Aces repeated their performance of the previous day in front of 10,000 enthusiastic supporters. Trevor expressed his pleasure at the support given to the Nortons by the crowd and his hat-trick of wins by standing on the footpegs of his machine and waving. While Trevor and Steve had been showing the opposition the way home, Robert had ventured over to Finland for the Kouvola circuit round of the TT F1 World Championship. In practice he came fourth but during the race he fell on lap nine and did not finish.

At the start of August the action moved to Donington Park for the British Grand Prix and round six and seven of the MCN TT Superbike series. On the Saturday

Trevor Nation lines up alongside 500 GP World Champion Eddie Lawson at the Save the Children Day, Brands Hatch.

Steve came fourth but Trevor broke down at Craner curves and had to watch as the race went on without him. On the Sunday Steve moved up to a hard-fought third place and Trevor came in fifth, having had to fight his way up from a poor start. Earlier in the day Trevor had fitted in two laps of the circuit, on a Commander with a young lady who had won a 'Pillion in a Million' competition with *Motor Cycle News*. Concerned that he should not frighten her, he carefully arranged the mirror so that he could see her face and watch the reaction; well, that was his story. At the same time tyre sponsors Michelin announced that they were withdrawing from road racing at the end of the season which meant that Barry Symmons was on the hunt for new tyres for next season. After four rounds of the championship, both Trevor and Steve were leading with 39 points, Rob McElnea was on 38 and Terry Rymer on 29 points.

The Ulster Grand Prix on August 11 at the Dunrod 7.5-mile course near Belfast was the final round of the TT F1 World Championship. Robert was there in company with Trevor. In the first race Robert came second and picked up seventeen points whilst his team mate failed to finish. Robert had scored 49 points from his races and finished in third place behind his brother Joey Dunlop on 54 points and the series winner on 60 points, Carl Fogarty, both riding Honda machines.

The bad luck that had haunted Trevor Nation during the 1989 season seemed to have left him and descended upon his team mate Steve Spray; at the rain soaked meeting at Thruxton (Trevor's home circuit) he came second and Steve finished 22nd. The race was delayed due to the changing weather conditions. The rain stopped and the track started to dry out–then it looked as if it would rain again. The frantic tyre changing was great entertainment for the spectators but not so enjoyable for the riders or their mechanics. When they did eventually start Steve and a number of other riders had decided to go out on intermediate tyres, whilst the rest had opted for full slicks. Unfortunately for some the choice of tyre proved to be wrong. On the rapidly drying surface Steve's tyres heated up too much and by lap four had begun to slide and on lap five the front went away before he could do anything about it. Fortunately he was not injured. During the race, led for the first three laps by Terry Rymer, Trevor managed to get ahead to the great delight of the crowd and was in the lead for two laps, even though his machine was obviously suffering a misfire. This ignition problem meant that Trevor could not accelerate smoothly out of the corners and he was overtaken by Rymer.

At Mallory Park on September 2 the Nortons were poised to challenge the opposition in front of 10,000-plus fans and a television audience. In front of the cameras, some riders try a little bit too hard and make mistakes that can affect other riders. This was the case for Trevor Nation who was shunted out of the race by

Things came right for Trevor Nation in 1990 after the frustration of the previous season.

Jamie Whitam at the hairpin on lap six. Earlier in practice Steve Spray was relegated to the fifth row of the grid by Paul Lewis who crashed into Steve and brought him down. Yet despite having to start from such a poor position Steve as usual fought hard to get toward the front and to the delight of the Norton fans managed to finish in eighth place.

A different challenge faced the riders on the south coast on September 8 with the Brighton Speed Trials, held on the sea front. Trevor was in his element performing wheelies at high speed. He turned the event into a demonstration of the Norton rotary, a display of breathtaking skill producing practice runs of 134.00 mph on one wheel only and winning with a terminal speed of 169.0 mph.

Oulton Park on September 22 witnessed another example of his return to form with rounds eight and nine of the MCN TT F1 series. In round eight Trevor had to contend with a powerful machine on a very slippery surface and wisely decided in the last few laps to settle for second behind the surprise winner John Reynolds on a Kawasaki. Team mate Steve did not fare so well and eventually retired. In the second race, which was nice and dry, Trevor was forced to retire with clutch problems and Steve finished in sixteenth place. The next day the team were at Cadwell Park for rounds ten and eleven and the weather was appalling with rain lashing down. In the wet Steve Spray made a magnificent start, closely pursued by Trevor and the rest of the pack but by lap two Steve was obviously suffering some sort of problem as he was caught and passed by Trevor and then by Ray Stringer. Never one to give up, Steve fought to keep up but in the short ten-lap race he was eventually beaten into fifth place. In the second race,

Trevor got a good start in second place and spent the rest of the race trying to get his machine to respond to enable him to close on the leader; but damp had obviously got into the ignition and he could not close the gap. Steve suffered a similar problem and ended the race in 11th place. For the King of Cadwell race it was again Steve who stormed into the lead, closely pursued by Trevor and the rest of the grid. Things appeared to be going right for him at long last: then on lap two, his intermediates lost their grip and he went down. Meanwhile, Trevor was fighting hard for his second place, not just for the race but also for championship points. Trevor needed those points, plus two more from the coming meeting at Brands hatch, to win the title, a good incentive that meant he fought off all the challenges, to hold onto second behind Carl Fogarty.

The next round of the Shell Oils Supercup (again televised) was held at Donington Park on September 30 in wet conditions. Trevor chose to go out on full wets which paid off at the start when he left the rest of the grid behind to set an early lead. Unfortunately, the rain had stopped and the track was rapidly drying out, which caused the tyres to overheat and begin to break up. A closing John Reynolds took advantage of this and took the lead on lap eight. Trevor was finding the machine more of a handful as the tyres came apart and he was passed by Carl Fogarty and Jamie Whitham, but managed fourth place. Steve also had problems throughout his race and ended up in twelfth place.

Kirkistown in an ex-airfield circuit of 1.49 miles in County Down Northern Ireland, was the venue for October 13. For the first time, three Norton race machines competed in the same race. Trevor was the most successful at this meeting where he finished a consistent fifth in all three races, Steve finished thirteenth, eleventh and tenth and Robert finished just behind Trevor in each race, sixth, seventh and sixth.

Brands Hatch Euphoria

The season drew to a close with the final leg at Brands Hatch and a huge crowd flocked to the meeting to see the Nortons and Trevor clinch the prestigious MCN TT Superbike Championship; with the added bonus of an appearance by Grand Prix rider Ron Haslam racing an RCW588 for the first time. This was not the first time that Ron had actually ridden the RCW588; he had first tried it out at Donington Park just before the British Grand Prix back in August, and had been suitably impressed with the machine.

For the Brands Hatch meeting Ron was brought in to assess the bike for competition. In practice on the

JPS O – Ron Haslam.

ABOVE **Ron gets a push to work. First time out at Brands Hatch he took ninth and then a creditable fifth place.**

LEFT **Colin Rust's Rotary sidecar (Photo: Eric Cavill).**

Saturday in dry sunny conditions Ron was circulating very quickly on a machine which carried 'O' on the number plates. He came into the pits regularly to consult with Ron Williams before shooting back out. Ron admitted afterwards that he was very impressed with the machine and thought that it had potential for Grand Prix application. He was thoroughly looking forward to racing the bike the next day.

On the Sunday the weather was cold and grey but it couldn't dampen Norton enthusiasm. Trevor only needed two points to win the prestigious MCN TT Superbike Championship and Steve and Ron were both looking for a win, especially in front of one of the biggest crowds at Brands Hatch for years, a guesstimated 25,000.

The race started with Ron and Trevor towards the front of the grid with Steve further back. The bitterly cold weather did not help, in that the tyres were slow to heat up; the suspension was also affected. On lap four the race was stopped after Iain Simpson collided with Ron Haslam coming out of Druids hairpin and tumbled down the track. Fortunately this looked worse than it was. When the race was re-started Terry Rymer shot away, chased hard by the following pack which gave the crowd some exciting racing. In the end Trevor finished in seventh place which gave him four points: he had won the championship. Ron finished in ninth place and Steve finished in sixteenth place. In the second race the pressure was off Trevor and he settled down to enjoy himself fighting for places with Tim Bourne and Mark Farmer, much to the delight of the crowd. Ron made a poor start but worked his way up through the field so that at the end of the race he crossed the line behind Trevor to take fifth place. Steve was obviously not happy and could only finish in seventeenth place. It should be remembered that Ron Haslam was riding the JPS Norton in his first competitive meeting and for the second time ever. With each race his confidence in the machine was obviously growing.

In the Superbike International race the crowd were on their feet cheering when on the fourth lap Ron slipped into third place and set off after Carl Fogarty and Terry Rymer, closely harassed by Rob McElnea. Trevor also made a good start and was chasing the leading four. The crowd was cheering and shouting practically throughout, asking the impossible. It was as if the Nortons had won when they crossed the line, Ron in third place and Trevor in fifth. Even Steve in 15th place was given a cheer. The Norton team had not won any races, Trevor had won the championship, Steve had come fifth, Ron had made an impression with his third place; and Barry Symmons actually smiled.

The 1990 season was wound up with a visit by Trevor Nation and Robert Dunlop to the Macau Grand Prix at the end of November. In the first leg on this road circuit Robert Dunlop finished fourth but Trevor could not make his front brake work effectively at one point and bounced off a wall sideways at around 20 mph. He remounted and charged through the field until halfway round the last lap, when he had problems with the rear wheel cush drive. In the second leg Trevor stormed through the pack and took over the lead on the second lap. He held this position until he was forced to retire on lap six when his engine overheated. Robert Dunlop was racing with a TV camera mounted on his fairing, but this worked loose and hampered him so much that he could only manage sixth place.

On reflection, the season had been one of mixed fortunes, Steve had started with high hopes of continuing his success but was plagued by a number of problems which for such a competitive rider must have been highly frustrating. For Trevor, after a slow start to the season he returned to his previous form which put him in consistent competition for the lead against the mighty Yamaha of Terry Rymer. On the World Championship Formula One scene Robert Dunlop had also done extremely well to finish in third place.

For 1991, Trevor Nation again carried the John Player Special colours on the rotary race machines in the Superbike and Supercup series, but his former partner, Steve Spray, had transferred to the Roton project. His replacement was 'Rocket' Ron Haslam, the Grand Prix rider. Ron was renewing his association with both Barry Symmons and Ron Williams with whom he worked whilst he was racing for the Honda Britain team during the early 1980s. In 1986, unable to secure Grand Prix rides with Honda Britain, he joined the French ELF Honda team of Serge Rosset to race their radically designed machine. This featured such things as an adapted MacPherson single arm front suspension, single arm rear suspension, and over the years a myriad different design ideas. Ron's skills as both a Grand Prix and development rider helped make the machine very competitive, and it was hoped that he could help achieve the same with the new machines that Ron Williams has developed for Norton.

Late in 1990 it was announced that to attract bigger grids, 750 cc four strokes plus the Nortons would be allowed to compete in the 500 cc Grand Prix series. Unfortunately, this decision was not approved by the FIM at their meeting in Geneva of January 19/20 1991, when they decided that it could be dangerous to mix machines of different performance.

At their spring meeting at the beginning of March the FIM came to a decision that to help boost the numbers on the Grand Prix grids they would allow rotary machines into the 500 cc races in 1991.

For the Norton factory the news came a little late and at the wrong time; the financial situation meant that there was insufficient money available for them to compete in more than one of the rounds. Team manager Barry Symmons felt that it would be better for them to concentrate on the original championships and then target the British Grand Prix round at Donington Park in August.

Sidecar Privateers

In 1989, sidecar racer Colin Rust was very impressed by the enthusiasm and interest shown by the crowd at Brands Hatch watching Trevor Nation and Steve Spray racing the John Player Special solos. 'I was inspired by the enthusiasm and interest of the crowds watching the Norton solos race. I thought if we could get a measure of that interest into sidecars it could only be good for sidecar racing in general.'

Most sidecar outfits today use Japanese high-performance two-stroke liquid-cooled engines and Colin felt that it might be good for sidecar racing if he could use a Norton rotary engine. Colin approached Norton to discuss the possibility of buying a rotary engine and getting suitable advice about setting the engine up for racing. Rust Racing was established and an engine purchased, most of the expense picked up by Colin himself. The engine that Norton provided was not the same as the ones used in the machines raced by Trevor Nation and Steve Spray, but one based upon the F1 588 cc liquid-cooled road bike. As Colin Rust describes it, 'It's a more refined version of the solo racer. It's fast and driveable and it's got the power characteristics of a two stroke and a four stroke. It's tractable as a four stroke but has no engine braking.' In addition to providing the engine, Norton also made the expertise of Brian Crighton available to the Rust Racing venture.

To house the engine Colin approached Terry Windle

Brian Crighton with Colin Rust and the Rotary engine he used.

of Windle Engineering, a specialist designer in Sheffield, and asked him to design a suitable chassis. To save weight but provide enough strength Terry suggested that the chassis should be constructed from sheet carbon fibre as a monocoque construction. The chassis was built by the Arrow F1 racing car team who are experts in carbon fibre construction.

In sidecar racing, the passenger is vital for keeping the outfit on the track, a rôle that is incredibly demanding both of skill and courage. One of the best passengers in sidecar racing is Tony Hewitt, former partner of Steve Webster. The duo were world champions many times during the 1980s. Tony decided that he would retire from racing at the end of 1989 season, but when approached by Colin his enthusiasm waxed once more. 'I'm in it for the interest really. Wouldn't have come back to racing for just anybody. I finished the GP racing because the challenge to win was gone. I wasn't getting that buzz anymore, it became a challenge to win again.' Having such a partner made an impact on Colin: 'I don't know he's there. It's great when you have a passenger you can put your full trust in.'

With the rotary engine installed in its purpose-built chassis the British outfit had its first public outing in June 1990 at the Cadwell Park circuit in the Shell Oils Supercup meeting. The appearance of the unique outfit was a great hit with the spectators, as Colin recalls, 'We did a couple of extra practice laps just for the crowd – they were on their feet cheering and waving.' During official timed practice the outfit qualified in sixth place behind some of the top outfits in this country. Unfortunately the first attempt ended in chaos. When it came to the race the outfit did not make the starting grid as on its way down the hill from the paddock the gear lever broke when they went over a bump.

There is no big sponsor backing the team at the time of writing and Colin has had to put his house on the market for the venture to continue; but it is hoped that a major investor can be found soon to allow this unique all-British venture to succeed.

The Penetrator: a glance at the list of sponsors reveals a great deal about the mechanical makeup of the machine.

The Penetrator Project

An unusual application was made of a works JPS rotary race engine, during the autumn of 1990, when it was loaned to Alex Macfadzean's Project Penetrator. Using the engine fitted into a cigar-shaped bodywork, an attempt was made on the British motorcycle land speed record. The record was held by Roy Daniels, who had set the record at 191 mph, on a twin-engined supercharged Triumph at the East Yorkshire airfield track at Elvington, in 1978.

Having carried out tests at the shorter track at Bruntingthorpe in Leicestershire, where an un-official time of 200 mph was achieved by rider Mick Booys, Alex Macfadzean was confident of breaking the record. Norton technician Dave Hickman attended the sessions to help set up the race engine for the project.

After several attempts at Elvington were aborted due to bad weather, on the very last run of the day the Penetrator ridden by Mick Booys succeeded in cutting through the cross winds to record a speed of 191.89 mph, a new 750 cc record.

The 1991 JPS Norton race team. With Steve Spray having moved on to Roton, Trevor Nation and Ron Haslam were looking towards Grand Prix racing. Though the season began clouded with uncertainty, and with the previous year's machines.

Trevor Nation

Height: 6 ft 1 in
Weight: 13 st 2 lbs
First race: 1978 on a machine built from a write-off
First success: 1979 North Gloucester Club Champion
Career highlights: 1990 Second, Senior TT
1989 Outright lap record holder Mallory Park
1986 1000 cc Production TT winner
1984 750 cc Production TT winner
Best moment: 'Winning a Superbike race at Brands Hatch in 1985.
I started in fifth or sixth place and after one of the hardest races of my life took the lead coming out of the last corner.'

Trevor Nation, known to his fans as 'Clever Trevor' was born in Taunton, Somerset. When he was young a picture of the great Italian ace Giaccomo Agostini at Deers Leap in the Isle of Man TT fired his interest. He began club racing in 1978 on a written-off machine that he prepared himself, 'I started club racing for fun, I did not think I would get anywhere to be honest.'

By 1983 Trevor had turned professional, racing with his own team. In 1987 he was offered a place with the Team Loctite Yamahas but was not really happy. At the end of that season he spoke to Brian Crighton at the racing show and was invited to attend a track session at Mallory Park to try the machine out. On the day, he and two other riders tried the machine and Trevor was going no faster than the others, until he asked for footpegs to be moved, after which he began to fly.

As result he was offered a place along with Simon Buckmaster to race the Norton rotaries in the forthcoming 1988 season. One of the reasons Trevor was so excited about the bike was that it was British. It is also important to Trevor that he gets to know the bike: 'I like to know my bike well, you have got to work together. The bike and you work as a team.'

He had a good season in 1988 followed by one that saw him suffer a number of injuries and breakdowns whilst his partner Steve Spray had a great season. During 1990, things gradually improved for Trevor and he finished the season by winning the MCN TT Superbike championship.

A hard competitor on the track, the big man with the wide grin is very popular with the fans with whom he takes time to talk. He delights in acknowledging the support from the crowd with 'wheelies' which he loves to perform. In his spare time he rides moto-cross, trials and push bikes. 'I live 25 miles from the factory and in the summer I will cycle into the factory and have a look to see what they are doing. It's the sort of thing I should be doing in the week to keep the old bones and heart ticking over.'

Steven Spray

Height: 5 ft 11 in
Weight: 10 st
First race: 1985 Cadwell Park
First success: 1986 British Clubmans
Championship race at Cadwell Park
Career highlights: 1989 Motorcycle Man of the Year
1989 British Formula One Champion
1989 ACU 750 cc Supercup Champion
1989 Lap records at Thruxton, Snetterton, Brands Hatch Indy circuit, Cadwell Park, Donington Park
1988 ACU Star 1300 cc Champion
1988 Winner on Norton debut – Powerbike International at Brands Hatch
1988 'Prince of Pembrey' Champion
1987 'Prince of Pembrey' Champion
1986 'Prince of Pembrey' Champion
Best moments: 'Winning the 1989 British Championship and Supercup series for JPS Norton.'

Steve Spray's home town is Gedling in Nottinghamshire where he joined the family transport business, Spray Transport, upon leaving school. He began racing in 1985 after the age of 22 and made rapid progress. In 1988 Steve had numerous wins on his RG500 Suzuki, promising great things for the future. His abilities had been well noted by Brian Crighton (amongst many others) so when Simon Buckmaster withdrew from the Norton team there was no hesitation in offering the machine to Steve. It led to a dream debut at the Powerbike International meeting at Brands Hatch in October 1988. He first rode the machine in practice on the Friday and them proceeded to improve his lap times on the Saturday and win the Formula One race, followed by the Powerbike International on the Sunday. 1988 was a great year as he also won the ACU 1300 cc Championship. The following season saw Steve smash a number of lap records and win two major championships.

At the time of writing, Steve is still riding a rotary-engined bike, but now for the Roton team with Brian Crighton.

Robert Dunlop

Height: 5 ft 4 in
Weight: 9 st
First race: Aghadowey 1978
First success: Manx GP Newcomers race 1983
Career highlights: 1990 Winner, North West 200
1990 Winner, Isle of Man TT 125 cc
1989 Winner, Isle of Man TT 125 cc
1989 Winner, Macau Grand Prix
1987 Enkalon Sports Personality of the Year
1986 Winner North West 200 Formula Two
1983 Winner John Player 125 Championship
1983 Winner Manx GP Newcomers race
Winner of Ulster and Irish Championship in every
class – 125 cc, 250, 350 and 1000
Best Moment: 'Winning the 1990 North West 200
for JPS Norton in my debut for the team.'

FIM

From the very beginning of the Norton rotary race machine's existence there has been controversy over the capacity rating of the engine, in comparison to reciprocating engines. When the machine was first raced at Darley Moor the ACU (Auto Cycle Union) the British governing body, were unsure of the capacity ruling so they placed a 1.7:1 rating on it, which made it 997 cc. The FIM (*Fédération Internationale Motocycliste*) decided that the capacity rating should be higher and so rated it at 2:1 or 1176 cc, basing their argument on the engine's cycle of phases. By the time the engine fires, the Technical Committee argued, it has already trapped a fresh charge of mixture. If this forms the basis of their decision it must surely follow that a two stroke should have a 2:1 rating, so a 250 cc would then be classed as a 500 cc. The insurance companies in this country, the Ministry of Transport and the police all accept that the Norton is rated as the company says, at 588 cc.

In October 1988 at the FIM Congress Norton was

granted a temporary rating of 1.7:1 as had been accepted by the ACU which allowed Norton to contest the F1 World Championship during 1989. But Norton wanted to compete at 500 Grand Prix level; as group Chief Executive Philippe Le Roux said, 'Norton wants to race at the highest level. We are involved in technical discussions with the FIM and our plans will be subject to their approval.'

In May 1989 Norton had to withdraw their new water-cooled machine from the first round of the F1 World Championship at Sugo in Japan. Not until the ACU had proof that Norton had manufactured two hundred water-cooled machines could they receive homologation approval for the machines to be raced. This raises another issue, in that two hundred machines are easy to produce for the Japanese manufacturers who produce machines on a large scale, but it is not so easy for a small concern like Norton.

The future of the 500 Grand Prix is now threatened: unless the TT Formula One type machines are allowed to compete, there will be too few entrants to fill the grid.

With pressure from both the Grand Prix organisers and the television companies, it is expected by most commentators that this suggestion will be adopted for all 500 Grand Prix races.

If this is the decision, Norton can go ahead with their long term ambition to compete in the GP Arena, but it must be remembered that these are early days for the rotary and they cannot be expected to go out and win against the two strokes immediately. A major factor is the tremendous cost of racing at this level. For Norton additional sponsorship on a large scale would be needed for them to appear on the same grid. A totally new rotary engine will have to be built, probably featuring fuel injection and an engine management system. To do this will probably cost several million pounds, so massive sponsorship will be required.

Will this be a Grand Prix sight in the near future? Norton vs the Japanese (in this case Yamaha).

1991

For Norton the 1991 season started with testing sessions at Mallory Park for Trevor Nation and his new team mate Ron Haslam. Practice commenced with the same machines raced the previous season as the new 1991 JPS Norton NRS588 being developed by Ron Williams was still not complete.

At the end of the previous season the race machines had been sold to a private collector who was keen to see the machines preserved for prosperity. Therefore Norton had to 'borrow' back two machines with which to start the season.

Norton were competing in the Supercup British Championship races, the MCN TT Superbike Races, several road races – including the Isle of Man – and to complete the racing calendar, a number of miscellaneous events. The major event must be the entry into the British Grand Prix, to be held at Donington Park on August 4, 1991. The first meeting for Norton was held at Donington where a massive crowed turned out to see Ron Haslam on the Norton racing on his home circuit. The occasion was the Diamond Jubilee TT F1 race. As Ron later admitted, his over revving of the engine off the line caused him to make a poor start as the rear wheel was spinning, reducing acceleration, but in a closely fought race he delighted the fans by making up ground and finishing in second place. Trevor was unhappy with the rear suspension of his machine during practice and this problem continued to plague him during the race, but despite this he finished in sixth.

The next race for Ron Haslam was at Pembrey, South Wales where he was primarily concerned in 'race' testing. Trevor's next meeting was at Castle Coombe. After a luckless nine months Trevor returned to winning form where in a closely contested race he regained the lead on the last lap and held on to win by four-fifths of a second from John Reynolds on a Kawasaki. The next day at his home circuit of Thruxton, the fast, flat circuit that ideally suits the Norton, he again came first. The race was stopped a lap early due to the treacherous condition of the surface after heavy rain. Action then moved north to Snetterton where in the televised Shell Oils ACU Supercup 750 cc TT F1 (held in brilliant sunshine) the Norton duo finished in fourth and fifth positions in the first race. Ron Haslam had started in pole position. This was despite the fact that Ron had developed an unusual noise in the engine during final practice prompting an engine strip and rebuild prior to the race. In the second race which was again hotly contested (fairing to fairing contact was a frequent occurrence) Ron Haslam was denied his first Norton win by 0.22 sec when Rob McElnea dived underneath at Russells and outgunned him to the line. Team mate Trevor Nation went out on a spare machine and unfortunately had to retire when in the leading group when his machine developed a misfire that left him with no power at higher revs.

For the past twenty years there has been an annual match between a British team and a team from the United States. The result of the match is determined from the results of six races. The races are split between two race circuits, in 1991 at Mallory Park on Sunday May 5 and Brands Hatch on the following day – Spring Bank Holiday. Norton's involvement had added importance as Ron Haslam was team captain of the twelve man British squad. Trevor was also in the team and pleased to represent his country in such an event, and have a chance to add to his wins so far.

The American team in this 20th anniversary year of the Anglo-American competition was led by triple world champion Freddie Spencer. At Mallory Park in the first race Trevor raced through to third place with Ron in sixth place, a result that was repeated in the second race. In the third race Trevor was highsided as he accelerated onto the main straight. He was smashed by the machine injuring his knee, yet he managed to hang onto the bike and get it back to the pits where he collapsed. Ron dropped a place in this third race but still gained eight valuable points for his team.

At Brands Hatch Ron fought a hard first race (despite being a team event, individual honours are still at stake) taking the lead on the last three laps to win. Fired by his first win on the Norton, Ron rode in determined style to a second win just ahead of Rob McElnea with whom he had continually changed places throughout the latter stages of the race. Trevor, still suffering from the previous day's mishap, managed twelfth, eighth and fifth place in Monday's racing. Ron finished third in the third race. The consistent high placings of the British team members gave them overall victory.

It must be remembered that the machines being raced were now in their third year, which is an extremely long time in racing. The massive Japanese investment in development means that their machines are continually being uprated. Speculation was growing over the new 1991 JPS Norton NRS588 (Norton Racing Services). Although this is a new machine it cannot be expected to go out and win straight away. Time is needed for riders to accustom themselves to the machine and for fine tuning and adjustments to be made.

ABOVE RIGHT **NRS588, photographed at Snetterton on its first outing in May 1991, with new Micron exhaust system.**

RIGHT **A toothed belt replaces the original chain primary drive. Kevlar-reinforced primary drive belt helps reduce any snatch in the transmission. (Photographs: Don Morley)**

1991 JPS NORTON NRS588

TECHNICAL SPECIFICATIONS

Engine:	Liquid pressure cooled twin-rotor rotary
Displacement:	588cc
Compression ratio:	9.2:1
Carburation:	Twin Keihin flat slide down draught
Ignition:	Norton reluctor triggered capacitor discharge
Tachometer:	Stack, 30 minute memory system
Gearbox:	Norton six speed, constant mesh
Clutch:	18 plate "wet" clutch using sintered bronze friction plates and diaphragm spring
Power output:	More than 135bhp at 9,800 rpm at shaft
Maximum torque:	78lbs/ft at 8,000 rpm
Frame:	Fabricated aluminium twin spar, designed by Ron Williams, fabricated by Harris Performance and assembled by JPS Norton Racing
Subframe:	Composite saddle
Suspension:	Front - White Power upside down forks
	Rear - Multiple cantilever single shock
Brakes:	Twin 310mm front discs with four piston one-piece Lockheed calipers
	Single 210mm rear disc with twin piston Lockhead caliper
Wheels:	3.75 x 17 three-spoke magnesium PVM front wheel
	6.00 x 17 three-spoke magnesium PVM rear wheel
Tyres:	Michelin radials
Weight:	Less than 135 kgs

ACTION MEDIA INTERNATIONAL LTD · DEENE HOUSE · MARKET SQUARE · CORBY · NORTHANTS NN17 1AA
TELEPHONE (0536) 400490 · FAX (0536) 202371

Norton NRS588 and Roton

It was at Snetterton that the new race machine was revealed for the first time during Friday afternoon's practice session, when the Norton riders took it round for several laps before it was put back in the team transporter. The machine would not be raced until it was felt that it was fully complete and ready for competition. In outward appearance it is a much slimmer machine than its forerunners. Amongst the visible changes are a Micron exhaust system and a toothed belt instead of chain primary drive.

Brian Crighton's Roton that went off to Australia to compete in the Eastern Creek Grand Prix to be ridden by Steve Spray on April 7 did not make such a dramatic entry into Grand Prix racing for the rotary engine as had been hoped. The machine was outclassed, but Steve Spray managed to take the machine across the line in fifteenth place to gain a first world point for a rotary-engined machine in Grand Prix competition, the first time that a British-designed machine has done so since 1974, when Selwyn Griffiths and Geoff Barry took ninth and tenth places in the Senior TT, (unfortunately not on Nortons but Matchless G50s).

At Oron Park in the Australian F1 Championship Grant Hodson (a former development rider with Bimota) won the two-part race. In the first race he was second, (beaten by 0.2 sec), with the fastest lap of the day.

The Roton and Brian Crighton returned to England on May 12 for further modifications, with the British Grand Prix the target. Grant Hodson was brought over to ride. The prospect of two rotary-powered machines on the grid is fascinating.

Project P55: the F1

The concept of the Norton F1 super sports machine originated with the client/consultancy relationship between the factory and design consultants Seymour-Powell (see Chapter Five). Seymour-Powell were brought in under the government funded, 'Support for Design' scheme, to assist Norton in adapting their new motorcycle to accept a water-cooled version of the rotary engine that they had had to develop to cure the overheating problems they had encountered. On starting their consultancy work Seymour-Powell quickly decided that it would be an inappropriate use of government funding for them to merely adapt the design style of what was clearly an already dated machine. They therefore proposed and carried out an in-depth review of the company and its operations. They made a number of suggestions in a report that was completed in September 1983 and which the Norton management at the time did not act upon. When Norton was taken over in the spring of 1987 by a consortium headed by Philippe Le Roux, the Seymour-Powell report came to light and they were re-engaged.

Second time around, the new Norton management was more receptive to suggestions to help turn the company around, enabling it to get back into producing quality motorcycles.

Whilst this was taking place, Norton had ventured back into racing with a police machine, but one that was being continually developed by Brian Crighton.

One of the many renderings or design sketches originally submitted by Seymour-Powell.

ABOVE Life-size design produced using tape, which allows for swift alteration.

BELOW A two-dimensional foam board model constructed to show form and ride position.

A very different sketch for
the F1 than the one on page
152. Note the name –
Rotech–1.

A variation along the same lines, perhaps a little closer to the final product. Seymour-Powell were not working to any technical specifications at this time but were simply playing with the image.

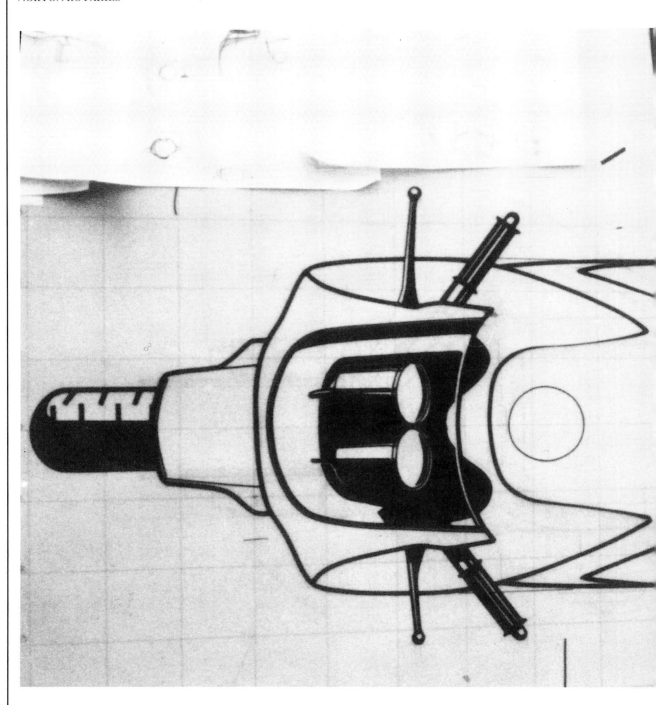

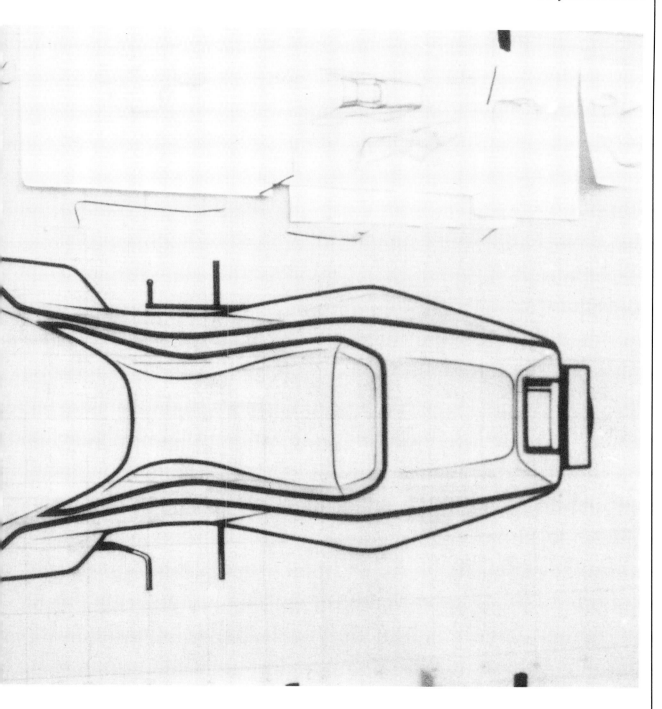

Full-size tape design from above. Note the grid for reference. The genuine shape of the F1 begins to appear.

ABOVE **Chassis used as the starting point for the clay model.**

OPPOSITE **The chassis is dressed with a wooden buck and fine clay is then added in layers (below) to form the machine with great accuracy.**

The machine used the air-cooled engine, the separate gear box and the monocoque chassis, but Brian Crighton had worked on the power output of the engine to make it more competitive. The management felt that the kudos of racing would be a powerful boost to the sales of the proposed sports machine that was envisaged in project P55. A racing programme would also prove useful in developing systems that could be carried over to the sports machine. It was hoped that through regular meetings with the race development team and the design consultants Norton could ensure that whatever was decided for the race machine remained appropriate for the P55.

While Norton was involved in a return to racing and was testing the reaction of the motorcycle market with the launch of the limited edition civilian machine, the Classic, Seymour-Powell were working on designing and developing a purpose-built police motorcycle, the Commander. Once the work on the Commander had been completed the new Norton management team was very keen to press ahead with the development of the P55 project, despite worries over the serious work load that this would impose. Delays of several months were caused by trying to finalise deals for government funding for certain aspects of the technical package.

In November 1987, the P55 project was finally given the okay. The brief was clear and simple: using the newly developed water-cooled engine and new chassis, design a new super sports machine to compete at the very top of the market, one which could capitalise on the successes achieved in racing.

Seymour-Powell established at the very beginning just what they envisaged for the machine: a single seater, with fully enclosed bodywork and an identity that would be akin to that of a Porsche, rather than following the fashion for race replicas, as had Honda, Kawasaki, Suzuki and Yamaha. The machine would also be as low as possible, with the smallest possible frontal area for effective aerodynamics. Visually, all the surfaces would flow into the next to form an almost seamless skin around the machine. The rear wheel area would also be brought into the styling and attention would be given to tidying up the air flow through the machine and out around the tyre. This gave rise to the upper and lower wheel fairings which visually integrated the wheel and its ancillaries. An added bonus for this form of styling was that it significantly reduced the spread of road dirt around the back of the machine and

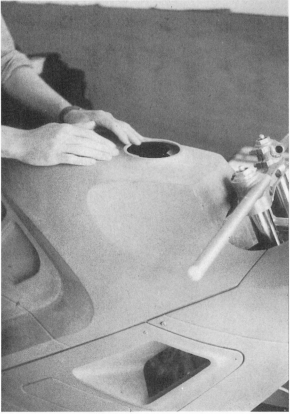

The model at this stage is extremely close to the look of the machine itself: compare the seat unit, fairing and overall dimensions with the real thing on page 167. Preparing a model like this is a hands-on, craftsman's job.

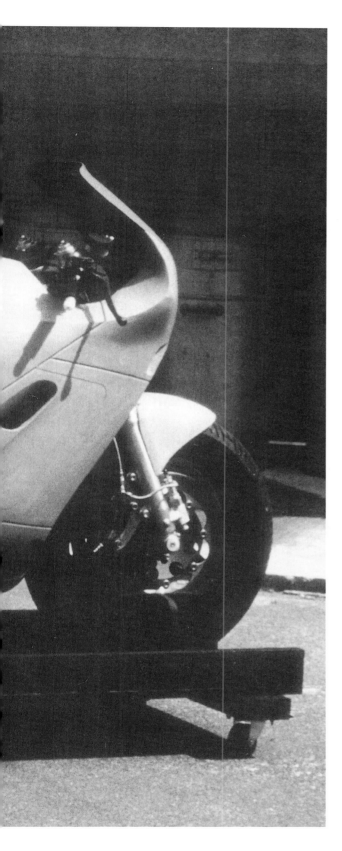

helped emphasise the aspect ratio of the rear tyre. With these ideas in mind a series of renderings, simple design sketches, were produced.

Having chosen a particular design the next stage was to make a life size tape design drawing. This involves drawing a life size representation of the motorcycle design using tape, which is a highly skilled technique. Minor modifications can be made quickly and easily to the drawing by lifting and repositioning the tape. Several views are made in this way; side view and a view from above are shown; (pages 153 and 158).

Using the tape design a china clay based card or rigid foam board is used to make another 2D representation, The material is used because it can be cut into and pieces can be stuck onto it easily. The next stage is to use special modelling clay on an actual chassis and wood buck, to allow the motorcycle to take form. One side is formed first and a grid is made from which form can be accurately transferred to the other side, ensuring exact symmetry. Once the basic structure of the machine has been formed, fine detail can be added. Details can then be painted onto the complete model which has an extremely fine surface finish. In the photograph it is difficult to believe that this is a clay model. The clay prototype of the machine was painted in a distinctive grey and red livery the night before it was wheeled across the road to its debut at the Motorcycle show at Earls Court.

After the model was shown at Earls Court Motorcycle Show in September 1988 (which resulted in a tremendous response from the trade, public and media), a detailed project specification and timetable of events was drawn up during January 1989. Several pre-production prototypes of the P55 were consequently

The finished model; finally, it's painted (above). Hard to believe this is wood and clay.

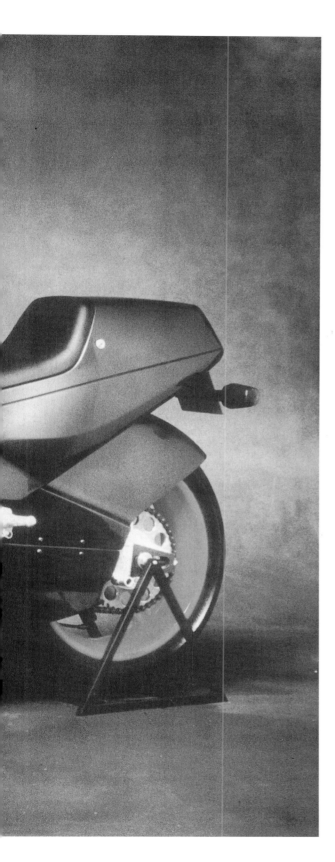

built for the International Motorcycle Show held at the NEC Birmingham on October 31 the same year. These were made available to the press for limited press coverage; it was from this point that the machine was officially launched and formal marketing took place. Prior to the launch it was decided that the P55 machine would be named the F1 and would adopt the distinctive black and gold livery of the race team sponsors, to celebrate the success of the John Player Special Nortons which had won the 1989 British Formula One Championship and the BBC Shell Oils Supercup.

When it appeared the machine was built around a twin-spar aluminium alloy beam chassis which had been tried and tested on the race track. It also shared an engine capacity of 588 cc but its engine operates in the reverse direction, (anti-clockwise) to the racer, with the intake and exhaust ports facing forwards and the spark plugs rearwards. The change was necessary so that a new gear box based around a Yamaha gear cluster could be used. It also gave rise to other benefits, in that it allowed the use of a shorter inlet tract for the Mikuni downdraft carburettors and a longer exhaust pipe to achieve the best balance between exhaust silencing and power output. The bodywork was formed by a one-piece unit manufactured by a local supplier. Race-bred 'White Power' front and rear suspension units ensured that the machine's handling capabilities matched its power output.

To reflect this racing theme, the early sales literature featured a picture of Steve Spray, wheelieing one of the race bikes under the title 'BITCH'. Inside the brochure was an annotated side-on shot of the F1 machine with the heading, 'SON OF A BITCH'. The desired association of racing machine and production motorcycle could not have been put more directly to the public.

Identifying the market

It goes without saying that Norton could not compete with the Japanese giants or BMW across the board: what they looked for – and found – was an exlusive niche, the very small volume 'superbike' market which would successfully display the advantages of the rotary engine, namely, its high power-to-weight ratio, high power-to-volume, its exceptional smoothness, the good torque characteristics and the reasonable fuel consumption. A supersports machine produced in small numbers should be able to commmand a price high enough to support the cost of research, manufacture, sales, and dealer margins.

The cost of the research, design and development

The F1 as it was presented at the Earls Court Show –
dark grey with red wheels.

ABOVE, LEFT TO RIGHT **P Morris, J Williams, D. Rawlings, S. Randall and F. Swift** pose with the F1 frame (Photo: J Noble, *Motor Cycle News*).

ABOVE RIGHT **The Norton F1 Superbike in racing livery.**

RIGHT **F1 bodywork for 'one of the most beautiful machines ever created'** (*Motor Cycle News*)

ABOVE LEFT **White Power** single shock unit.

LEFT **Sub-frames** awaiting assembly.

TOP **The F1 chassis** awaits clothing.

RIGHT **PVM wheel fitted** with Michelin radial sports tyre.

ABOVE The Yamaha/Lucas electrical system laid out prior to fitment.

LEFT The oil pump before its cover is fitted.

ABOVE RIGHT James Tildesley (left) and Philippe Le Roux OBE.

budget was in the region of £500,000 to which add prototyping fees of a further £60,000. This is chicken-feed to Honda, the project was not without risks to such a small and rapidly expanding concern. Demands on cash flow were so high that great emphasis had to be placed on generating funds from all Research and Development work carried out for various clients. But if sales of the machine failed to generate sufficient funds to cover the investment, it would have to be written off against other Norton business and that could well jeopardise the existence of the company.

It was calculated that sales of 500 motorcycles in the first year would enable the company to recover its development, engineering and capital investment in the project. A price of £12,700 was eventually set. Hopes were high for the new model. The projections forecast that a 100% increase in the sales of Norton motorcycles could be achieved. To do this it would have to exceed 30% penetration into a market area dominated by the race replica machines of Honda, Kawasaki, Suzuki, Yamaha and Bimota. The number of machines invol-

ved would have little impact on the world market sales of motorcycles but that particular market factor would be rocked.

By this time, manufacture of production quantities was well in hand but unfortunately, because of the complexities of the machine, initial quantities from production tooling were not available until April 1990.

In commercial terms there was little reaction to the price of the machine especially when it was compared to the price of Japanese or Italian equivalents such as the Yamaha FZR750R (OWO1), priced at £13,700, or the Bimota YB6 Tautara at £17,500!

From a United Kingdom-only launch, on opening the order book the response was gratifying, to say the least. Within weeks firm orders had been placed through the limited dealer network or through the factory itself for over one hundred machines. Sales forecasts for the period April 1990 to May 1991 required a minimum total of 200 units per year from all territories. Based upon these early UK sales and the worldwide interest provoked by the launch of the

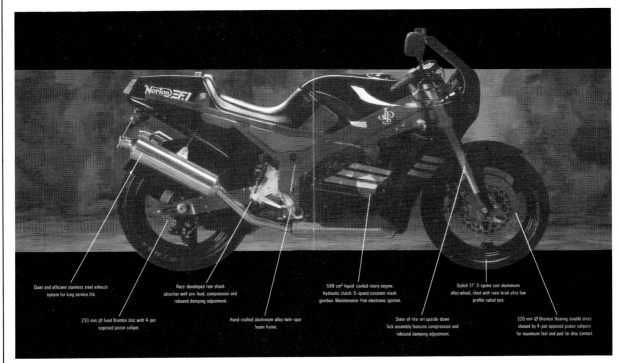

Quiet and efficient stainless steel exhaust system for long service life.

Race-developed rear shock absorber with pre-load, compression and rebound damping adjustment.

588 cm³ liquid-cooled rotary engine. Hydraulic clutch. 5-speed constant-mesh gearbox. Maintenance-free electronic ignition.

Stylish 17" 3-spoke cast aluminium alloy wheel, shod with race-bred ultra low profile radial tyre.

230 mm Ø fixed Brembo disc with 4-pot opposed piston caliper.

Hand-crafted aluminium alloy twin-spar beam frame.

State-of-the-art upside-down fork assembly features compression and rebound damping adjustment.

320 mm Ø Brembo floating double discs slowed by 4-pot opposed piston calipers for maximum feel and pad-to-disc contact.

BELOW The F1 brochure begins with the racing machines, a well-worn marketing ploy that in this case makes sense.

ABOVE 'Son of a bitch', as annotated in the brochure.

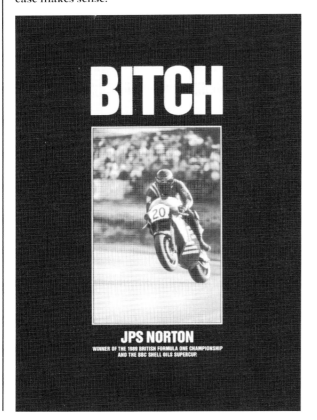

BITCH

JPS NORTON
WINNER OF THE 1989 BRITISH FORMULA ONE CHAMPIONSHIP AND THE BBC SHELL OILS SUPERCUP.

machine, Norton anticipated that orders from abroad, in particular Germany, Japan and the Unites States, will boost sales figures well beyond initial targets and create a waiting list for this highly priced but very desirable machine.

One of the first press reports on the F1 pre-production prototypes was prepared by Chris Dabbs who worked for *Motor Cycle News*. His reaction was extremely favourable.

The Norton F1 is one of the most beautiful looking machines ever created, with its smooth curves flowing into the next to create a composite package of a machine. The distinctive livery emphasises the physical neatness yet declares its racing pedigree connections with the JPS sponsored race team. With this machine you pose! It is an ego booster. Wherever you go people will stop, look and then look again but watch out for the talkers. They will want to know all about it, usually in detail!'

'We believe Britain can once more offer the best motorcycles in the world', said Mr Le Roux. 'We have chosen to innovate rather than imitate. It has been a difficult path to follow at times, but the Norton F1 is proof that British technology and British engineering is still the best in the world. The British motorcycle industry has been through difficult times in the last 30 years. We are proud that Norton and the Norton F1 machine will lead that industry into a new era.'

The Future

Norton launch biggest range

At the International Motorcycle Show at Birmingham's National Exhibition Centre on December 3, 1990, Norton exhibited their biggest ever range of rotary powered machines and model variants. With the continued growth in the motorcycle division, Norton announced an extended dealer network of eleven distributors in the UK. This is to complement the original sales operation that continues from the factory at Shenstone. Following the success of the F1 sports machine, a derivative of the championship-winning RCW588, Norton displayed a new variation of the model. At the show a metallic lilac model showing a number of cosmetic differences introduced the new free customised single or metallic colour option available.

The new Classic was launched as a limited edition machine. Only 100 machines were to be produced and these would be a water-cooled version of the original air-cooled model that first appeared in 1987 and was sold out within the first few weeks. This time around, however, there was to be no rush to buy and this Classic was quietly dropped, at least temporarily.

A new Commander that featured detachable Krauser panniers as original equipment also attracted a lot of attention from the touring rider visitors to the show. The well-made German luggage come in a range of sizes, from 25 to 42 litres. Special care had been taken to ensure that the pannier mounting brackets were fully integrated into the rear of the machine so that if the panniers were removed the machine maintained smooth lines. The panniers were very easy to fit or

(*continued p 182*)

Philippe Le Roux

Philippe Le Roux was born in London but raised in South Africa. In 1974 he returned to the UK to study Economics at the University of London before pursuing a career in banking. From 1976 until 1978 he was Industrial Analyst, Automotive Sector for the Bank of Montreal. He then went to work for the World Bank in Washington. There he was responsible for projects based in South and East Africa. From 1983 to 1986 he expanded his financial skills by working for a merchant bank specialising in corporate finance. In 1987 he became Managing Director of the group which bought Norton from the enthusiastic Manganese Bronze Chairman, Dennis Poore. Philippe says that taking over Norton from him was like taking on a personal crusade to make a future for the company using the rotary.

The saving grace of the Norton company was its name. This was recognised as a major marketing asset by Philippe Le Roux and realising that the name meant nothing without the motorcycle business he went back to the liquidators to acquire this. By February 1987 he was able to announce that the NVT group were purchasing Norton Motors.

After a review of Norton on his takeover he brought in outside consultants to advise him. He then decided to test the reaction of the buying public to the rotary engine with the Classic. Expansion into the motorcyle market and aero-engine market resulted in the company gradually increasing its profits.

Philippe was also determined that Norton should return to racing, as he saw this as a valuable promotional activity. He was able to use enthusiasm from within the company to effect the emergence of the Norton race team which then gained valuable sponsorship from Imperial Tobacco.

In recognition of his work in developing the Norton group and in particular the re-establishment of a British motorcycle manufacturing concern, Philippe Le Roux was awarded an OBE, and award shared he insists, by everyone involved with the work on the rotary engine.

As important as the motorcycle business is, Philippe Le Roux sees the main area of future development to be in other applications of the rotary engine such as aviation, leisure products and portable power or pumping uses.

He stood down as Chief Executive in 1991 when the recession began to rock the company; he had always insisted that one of his major ambitions was to see a British bike on the grid of the British Grand Prix, which would happen, sadly, very soon after his stepping down, at Donington Park in 1991.

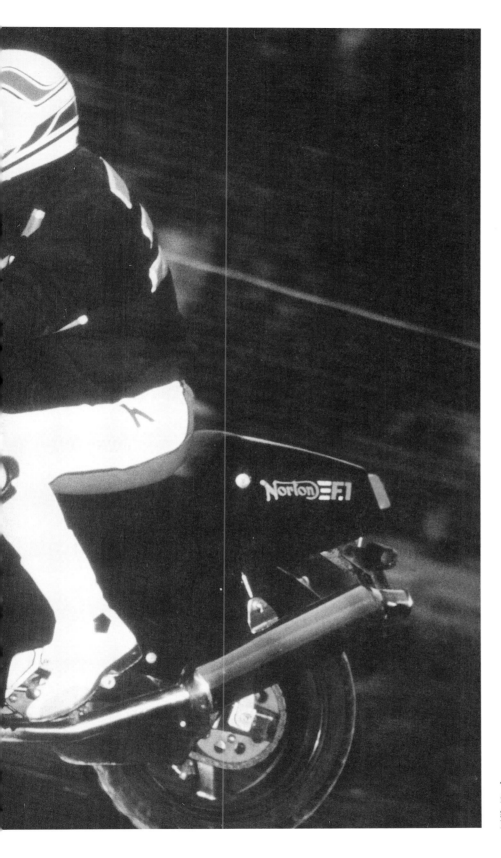

The author aboard his favourite machine at a greasy Brands Hatch, November 1990.

Graham Williams

Graham Williams is the Managing Director of Norton Motors Ltd who before joining the company had been the Director of an Armstrong components factory and also the Commercial Director of Mirrlees Blackstone Ltd.

From 1974 to 1982 he was the Managing Director of the specialist and light aircraft engine division of Rolls-Royce Motors with responsibility for technical and quality control for all diesel, petrol and multiple fuel engines manufactured by Rolls-Royce for the military and commercial markets. This responsibility also included the light aircraft engines manufactured under licence from Teledyne Continental Motors in the US. The development and certification of new aircraft engines produced by Rolls Royce was also part of the job brief.

Graham Williams is a Chartered Engineer with a wide range of general management experience including the development of products, market diversification, improving quality control and profitability of engineering businesses within fields of operation similar to that of Norton Motors Ltd.

'We have designed the F1 to be the best supersports machine in the world. It continues Norton's commitment to the rotary engine technology that has made us world leaders in the field and will be one of the most exlusive machines on the road.'

LEFT the F1 in red, at the International Motorcycle Show, Birmingham 1990. The padded seat snaps off for access to the oil tank and storage space.

THIS PAGE Commander with Krauser panniers at the same show.

ABOVE Norton Commander paramedic machine, developed initially for the West Midlands Ambulance Service.

RIGHT The F1R, a seductive package for the race privateers, with racing brake callipers and discs, six speeds and mag wheels. Initial output would be 12 machines, with others built specifically to order. Price for the out-of-the-box racer: £27,000.

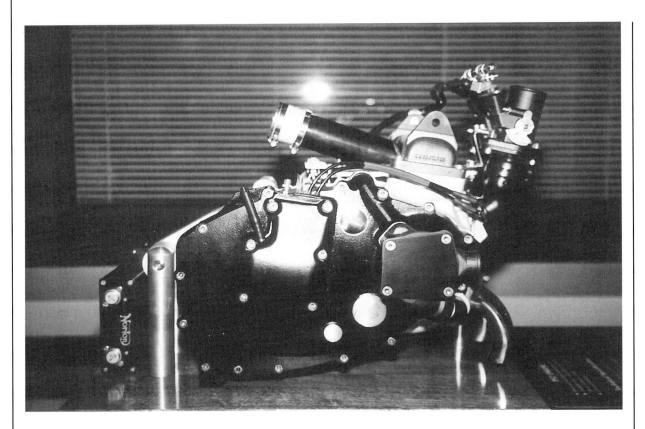

The P57 engine unit, available for side-car competition.

remove from the machine and could be used at high speed with no apparent effect on stability. Purchasers of the Commander could have a wider choice of colours with the new 'Candy Apple Red' and a 'Metallic Blue' option available.

Norton also exhibited a paramedic version of the patrol Commander that has been specially developed with the West Midlands Ambulance Service. A pilot scheme was carefully monitored to show that Norton mounted paramedics can significantly reduce the response time to incidents. The paramedic machine had been carefully furnished with a comprehensive range of medical equipment to cope with most situations. This was backed up by a short-wave communications package all fitted into its custom-built bodywork and mounted on a Commander to provide efficient transport to accident scenes. During the course of the show the West Midlands Ambulance Service took delivery of a third paramedic machine.

The F1R

For a long time the RCW588 has been the envy of many racers, so Norton announced that for the 1991 race season they would make available a race version of the F1, the F1R. The competition machine would be made in two versions, one with FIM-homologated specification, with flat slide carburettors and the other with

Weber–Alpha race-developed electronic fuel injection and an electronic engine management system. Another feature of this engine was an oil separator to remove oil from the coolant air to prevent it being lost to the outside. It works by condensing the oil from the hot, oil-laden air using a steel mesh. The oil then runs to the bottom of the separator and can be re-used. Standard specification for these machines would include a six speed gearbox, magnesium wheels, Lockheed Racing brake callipers and racing brake discs. To meet the FIM noise regulations the exhaust would be fully silenced.

Because the exhaust ejector system means of cooling as used in the race bikes is dependent on an unrestricted exhaust, silencing is a problem. Power development using this system is limited by this factor for race track noise limits have been reached already. Therefore the fan-cooled engine has been developed as it offers scope for further power development without an increase in noise. This new engine was exhibited for the first time at the show and featured a centrifugal fan which blows cold air through the engine.

For those wishing to set up their own machine, competitors would be able to buy a race-bred version of the F1 engine unit as a separate item complete with all its ancillaries. This compact twin unit, the P57, with its robust gearbox, would be aimed particularly at the side-car class. The limited production of this 130 bhp unit, that has scope for raising the power output to around 150 bhp, would be available from the spring of 1991 and be backed with technical support and advice from the factory.

Just before Christmas 1990, Norton were faced with the fact that due to the recession and a disastrous lack of attendance at the NEC Motorcycle Show, where too few orders for new machines were taken, they had to make a large number of staff cuts in the motorcycle division. In addition, the lack of orders for the new Classic that had been launched at the show resulted in it being withdrawn before it went into production.

A further blow to company morale came when the Department of Trade and Industry announced that they would be conducting an investigation into the company. They would be looking at all the activities of the Norton Group: this includes other companies such as Pro-fit an American pipe fittings firm, Minty the furniture making company and the recent controversial purchase of the German fastenings firm FUS. The investment in other companies had been seen as one of the ways that cash could be generated to develop the rotary engine business of Norton Motors. This side of the group business has been extremely costly on investment and has yet to make a profit. The outcome of the Department of Trade and Industry enquiry is not expected for some time.

So with the financial dealings of the Norton group exposed to the scrutiny of the national press Philippe Le Roux decided that it would be in the best interests of all the parties involved if he resigned as Chief Executive. He therefore handed over control of the company he resurrected to James Tildesley, the former non-executive chairman.

A number of changes were announced at the end of April, designed to get Norton back on a stable footing to carry them through these troubled times. A new Chief Executive, David McDonald, formerly of Advanced Material Systems, headed a new team that replaced the previous board of directors. David McDonald believed that a more realistic approach to motorcycle manufacturing along similar lines to those used by Triumph and backed by a complete dealer network was essential. To date the motorcycle division had not been cost effective and took second place to the company's aero-engine business; but for the future, motorcycle manufacture would spearhead the company's efforts. Another major step would be to make the rotary-engined motorcycles more competitively priced. To do this they would need to lower the price of all the machines – including the F1 – to one more akin to Japanese machines. Improvements would also be made to the Commander to enhance its true potential as a sports/tourer and the sale of the Commando twins spares business to the newly formed BSA group was planned.

Despite the gloomy outlook, Norton still believe they hold the future in their hands, in the shape of the Norton rotary engine; an audacious technological gamble that brought engineering pride back to the British motorcycle industry.

Appendices

Technical Specification: Classic

Engine		Twin chamber air cooled Norton rotary
	Chamber capacity	588 cc
	Power output	79 bhp π 9000 rpm
	Compression ratio	7.5 to 1
	Fuel	97 RON 4 star petrol
	Plus facility to use	91 RON 2 star petrol
Carburettors		SU H1F4 constant vacuum
	Needle	51 XA
	Spring	RED
	Choke size	$1\frac{1}{2}$ in diameter
Gearbox		Constant mesh
	Gear ratios	1st 12.4:1
		2nd 8.82:1
		3rd 6.72:1
		4th 5.71:1
		5th 4.8:1
Transmission	Primary chain	Duplex $92 \times \frac{3}{8}$ in pitch
		30 tooth engine sprocket
		57 tooth clutch sprocket
	Rear chain	Single row 112, 5/8 × 3/8 in
		Grand Prix chain 17 tooth
		gearbox sprocket 43 tooth
		rear wheel sprocket
	Overall gear ratio	(Using 4.8:1 final drive)
		15.6 mph π 1000 rpm
		in 5th gear
Clutch		18 plate diaphragm spring type, cable operated
	Material	Sintered bronze engaging with steel intermediate plates
Ignition	Spark Plugs	Two 10 mm surface gap non-adjustable type with long life platinum centre electrode Champion U.G. 80 P.V.
	Coils	Two 12 volt coils
	Ignition unit	Electronic Inductive
	Ignition	Electromagnetic
	Trigger unit	Contactless
Suspension	Front	Telescopic Forks 38 mm ($1\frac{1}{2}$ in) diameter tubes with 130 mm ($5\frac{1}{8}$ in) movement Oil capacity 250 cc each

Suspension	Rear	Koni gas/hydraulic adjustable pre-load and damping
Brakes		Hydraulically operated Twin front disc 280 mm (11 in) diameter Single rear disc 280 mm (11 in)
	Discs	Cast Iron
	Hydraulic fluid	DoT 4 or equivalent
	Calipers	Twin piston
Wheels	Front	WM2 (1.85) × 18 in
	Rear	WM3 (2.15) × 18 in Quickly detachable Cast aluminium
Tyres	Front	100/90 V 18
	Rear	120/80 V 18 V rated Pirelli Phantom MT 29 Front ribbed MT 28 Rear block
General	Kerb weight	227 kg (498 lbs)
	Fuel Tank Capacity	18 litres (4 Imp. Gals)
	Length	2180 mm ($85\frac{1}{2}$ in)
	Wheelbase	1486 mm ($58\frac{1}{2}$ in)
	Handlebar width	730 mm (28 in)
	Ground clearance	165 mm ($6\frac{1}{2}$ in)
Electrical Equipment	Battery	12 v 14 a.h.
	Alternator	3 ph. 220 W
	Horns	Twin Electromagnetic

Technical Specification: Commander

Engine Type		Liquid-cooled twin rotor Norton rotary
	Displacement	588 cc
	Compression ratio	9:1
	Maximum power	85 bhp (63.4 kW) at 9000 rpm
	Maximum torque	55.6 Ft/lbs (75.4 Nm) at 7000 rpm
	Carburation	2×38 mm SUH1F4 Constant vacuum carburettors
	Lubrication	Total loss with oil bath primary chain
	Engine Oil Capacity	4.45 Litres SAE 40 API/CC
	Fuel	Leaded or unleaded Min 95 Octane RON
Transmission	Primary drive	Duplex roller chain with hydraulic tensioner
	Clutch	Wet multi-plate disc/cable operated
	Secondary drive	$5/8 \times 3/8$ roller chain in sealed oil bath
	Secondary reduction ratio	17/43
Electrical	Ignition	(CDI) Capacitor Discharge Ignition
	Generator/Output	A.C. 3 phase Alternator generator/370 Watt
	Battery capacity	12 v 28 A.h. Two batteries fitted as standard
	Headlight	12 v 60/55 W
	Daylight running lights	Two 12 v Sealed Units
Chassis	Overall Length	2200 mm
	Overall Width	880 mm
	Overall height	1470 mm
	Seat height	830 mm
	Wheelbase	1486 mm
	Minimum Ground Clearance	180 mm
	Dry weight	235 kg
	Fuel capacity	23 Litres
	Frame type	Pressed steel monocoque
	Front wheel	MT 2.15×18 in Cast Aluminium
	Rear wheel	MT 2.75×18 in Cast Aluminium
	Front Wheel Travel	145 mm
Tyres	Front	100/90 V 18 in Tubeless Standard fitment Pirelli Phantom
	Rear	110/90 V 18 in Tubeless Standard fitment Pirelli Phantom
Brakes	Front	Twin 265 mm discs with opposed piston calipers
	Rear	Single 265 mm disc with opposed piston caliper

Standard Equipment
Day time running lights
Double stop/tail/rear fog lamps
Analogue speedometer/electric tachometer/fuel level gauge/digital clock
Headlamp main beam indicator lamp/oil level warning light/direction
Indicator repeater lights/neutral indicator light
Radio console recess
Twin 25-litre lockable panniers
Twin rear view mirrors
Adjustable footrest position
Adjustable handlebar position

Warranty   Twelve months unlimited mileage
A number of local authorised Norton service dealers are being established throughout the country at the time of writing to ease servicing, but advice on any aspect of the machine is always available from the factory.

Technical Specifications: F1

Engine Type

	Twin chamber liquid-cooled Norton rotary
Displacement	588 cc
Compression ratio	9:1
Maximum power	95 PS DIN (69.9 kW) π 9500 rpm
Maximum torque	57 lbs/ft (77.3 Nm) π 75000 rpm
Carburation	Twin 34 mm Mikuni BDS downdraft carburettors
Lubrication system	Total loss
Engine oil capacity	2.4 Litres
Fuel	20-litre capacity of Minimum 95 RON leaded or unleaded

Transmission

Primary drive	Twin simplex roller chains with hydraulic tensioner
Clutch type	Wet, multi-plate
operation	Hydraulic
Secondary drive	5/8 × 3/8 in 'O' ring chain
Primary reduction ratio	1.781:1
Secondary reduction ratio	2.529:(17/43)
Gearbox	Five speed constant mesh
Gear ratios	1st 2.571:1
	2nd 1.778:1
	3rd 1.381:1
	4th 1.174:1
	5th 1.037:1

Electrical

Ignition	Electronic inductive discharge
Generator	370 W ACG
Battery capacity	12 volt 14 A.h.
Headlight	12 v 60/55 W H4

Chassis

Overall length	2100 mm
Overall width	900 mm
Overall height	1110 mm
Seat height	750 mm
Wheelbase	1440 mm
Rake	25 Degrees
Trail	99 mm
Minimum ground clearance	175 mm
Dry weight	192 kg
Fuel capacity	20 litres
Frame type	Twin spar aluminium alloy beam
Front wheel	MT 3.5 × 17 cast aluminium
Front wheel travel	110 mm
Front suspension	White Power upside-down forks, compression and rebound damping adjustable
Rear wheel	MT 5.50 × 17 cast aluminium
Rear wheel travel	143 mm
Rear suspension	White Power single shock, pre-load, compression and rebound damping adjustable

Tyres

Front	Michelin 120/79 ZR 17 in Radial (tubeless)
Rear	Michelin 170/60 ZR 17 in Radial (tubeless)

Brakes

Front	Twin 320 O floating Brembo discs with 4-pot opposed piston calipers
Rear	Single 230 mm O Brembo disc with 4-pot opposed piston caliper

Equipment	Speedometer	
	Tachometer	
	Temperature gauge	
	Warning lights	
Warranty	Motorcycle	One year, unlimited mileage, parts and labour
	Engine core	Three years, unlimited mileage, parts and labour (excludes transmission and gearbox)

Production Figures

Classic: 105 sold. 5 extra were produced, but not released to the public.

Interpol II: 350. 200 were taken up by the police and RAC, 150 were purchased by the MoD.

Commander: 253.

F1:   205 to June 1991.

Index